SECRETS of a CIVIL WAR SUBMARINE

SOLVING THE MYSTERIES OF THE *H. L. Hunley*

SALLY M. WALKER

CAROLRHODA BOOKS · MINNEAPOLIS

For all trailblazers—past, present, and future—who show devotion to their chosen field of work

. . . .

While writing about the *H. L. Hunley,* I went on several marvelous research journeys. Fortunately, my cruises with the *Hunley* were happy ones—due largely to the members of the current *Hunley* crew. Many thanks to Maria Jacobsen, Harry Pecorelli III, Shea McLean, Claire Peachey, Paul Mardikian, Linda Abrams, Doug Owsley, and Senator Glenn McConnell for patiently answering a boatload of questions. Additional thanks to Kellen Correia for providing contact information and coordinating the complex process of gathering photographs, and to Brian Hicks for sharing his *Hunley* knowledge. One evening during one of my visits to Charleston, I sat on Adger's Wharf and watched the sun set. I like to think that James McClintock, John Payne, Horace L. Hunley, George Dixon, and their crews sat there with me. Without them, there would be no story. —S. M. W.

Text copyright © 2005 by Sally M. Walker
Illustrations and maps on pp. 7, 13, 15, 17, 18, 19, 36, 80 by Laura Westlund © 2005 Lerner Publishing Group, Inc.

Carolrhoda Books®
An imprint of Lerner Publishing Group, Inc.
241 First Avenue North
Minneapolis, MN 55401 USA

For reading levels and more information, look up this title at www.lernerbooks.com.

Library of Congress Cataloging-in-Publication Data

Walker, Sally M.
    Secrets of a Civil War submarine : solving the mysteries of the *H. L. Hunley* / by Sally M. Walker.
      p.   cm.
    Includes bibliographical references and index.
    ISBN-13: 978–1–57505–830–6 (lib. bdg. : alk. paper)
    ISBN-10: 1–57505–830–8 (lib. bdg. : alk. paper)
    1. H. L. Hunley (Submarine) 2. Submarines (Ships)—United States—History—19th century. 3. United States—History—Civil War, 1861–1865—Naval operations—Submarine. 4. Charleston (S.C.)—Antiquities. 5. Excavations (Archaeology)—South Carolina—Charleston. I. Title.
    E599.H4W35 2005
    973.7'57—dc22   2004019646

Manufactured in the United States of America
13-52922-7573-5/13/2022

Contents

A Lost Treasure

For more than one hundred years, a submarine lay buried beneath the ocean floor near Charleston, South Carolina. The H. L. Hunley *was no mere shipwreck. She was a secret weapon—an engineering marvel of the Civil War and the first submarine to sink an enemy ship. Her daring exploits included tragedy, success, and a mighty explosion. But during her historic final mission in 1864, something went disastrously wrong. The* Hunley *never returned to port. Instead, she rested quietly, a silent tomb visited only by fish and other sea creatures.*

The Hunley *lay untouched for so long not because she had been forgotten, but because she couldn't be found. Divers began searching for her days after her disappearance. Sailors dragged the ocean floor with anchors and chains. Some of these people wanted to find the submarine to learn about her innovative machinery. Others hoped she would make them rich—especially after the 1870s, when circus owner P. T. Barnum offered a $100,000 reward for her recovery.*

Over the years, some divers claimed to have found the Hunley, *but none could prove their discovery. The ocean kept the submarine's location a secret. At first, murky water and white-capped waves hid her from view. Then, inch by inch, swirling sand and mud covered her iron hull. The* Hunley *disappeared from sight, buried beneath a blanket of silt.*

For 131 years, the submarine's secrets remained concealed. In 1995 her story took a startling turn. As she had during the Civil War, the Hunley *again made newspaper headlines. How the* Hunley *came to be on the ocean floor, how she came to leave it, and what happened next make up one of the most compelling stories in the history of archaeology and the history of the Civil War—an amazing tale of bravery, mystery, bones, and gold.*

Chapter One
A Seafaring Stealth Weapon

By August 1863, the people of Charleston, South Carolina, knew hardship.
The Civil War, raging for almost two and a half years, had become part of
everyday life. Gunshots regularly peppered the air. Exploding mortars shook
people awake at night. Fire had gutted the heart of the city, destroying
hundreds of homes and businesses.
The war had taken a heavy toll.

The residents of
Charleston—poor and rich,
enslaved and free—suffered
from attacks that left parts
of the city in ruins.

The greatest danger floated just outside
Charleston Harbor. On President Abraham
Lincoln's orders, Union warships patrolled the
surrounding seas, forming a blockade that
trapped Confederate ships at port and prevented
incoming ships from docking. Charleston was
one of the South's biggest and busiest port cities.
In better times, its harbor had been a bustling
center of trade. But under the blockade, ships

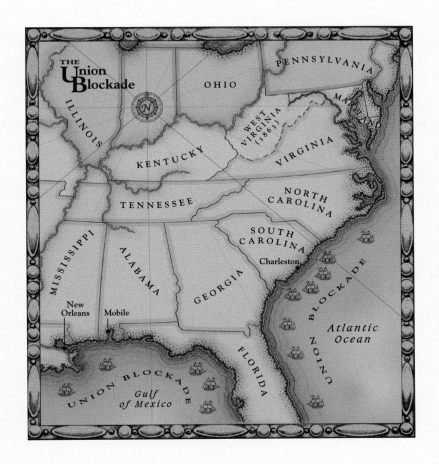

carrying trade goods could no longer enter or leave the harbor. Ships carrying guns, gunpowder, and shipbuilding materials—all desperately needed by the Confederate military—could no longer reach shore.

Slowly but surely, the blockade was strangling the Confederacy. The South's chances of winning the war grew dimmer every day the Union vessels remained in place. Clearly, the Confederacy needed to destroy the blockade and open Charleston and other Southern ports. With few ships capable of challenging a Union warship, the Confederate navy had to rely on another means, an underwater explosive called a torpedo.

Civil War torpedoes had enough power to blow up a ship, but their success was far from guaranteed. A modern torpedo contains a propeller that pushes it through the water toward an enemy target. During the Civil War, torpedoes lacked this technology. Some didn't move at all; they were anchored to the bottom in harbors and river channels. An electric cable ran from the torpedo to shore. When an enemy ship sailed close to the torpedo, a lookout man on land triggered the explosion. If his timing was just right, the ship could be damaged, perhaps even sunk. Many times, though, the explosion occurred too late—or not at all if the cable or torpedo malfunctioned.

Other torpedoes floated loosely in the water. They contained a mechanism that exploded when the torpedo bumped into another object—hopefully an enemy ship.

But no one could predict when or if such an explosion would occur. While torpedoes helped discourage Union ships from venturing too far into a harbor or up a river, they weren't effective weapons for breaking the blockade.

A third way to deploy a torpedo was to deliver it directly to the target. The Confederate navy used boats called Davids for this purpose. A David was a cigar-shaped wooden boat powered by a steam engine. Part of its hull was clad with iron sheeting. A polelike device called a spar stuck out from the front of the boat; the torpedo was fitted near the end of the spar. Protected by her iron armor, a David would steam up to an enemy vessel and ram the spar through the ship's hull. A crewman would trigger the explosion by pulling a lanyard, or long rope, after the David backed away from the ship.

The Davids did successfully deliver and explode torpedoes. But it wasn't easy. In daylight a David's smokestack and iron sheeting were easily spotted. At night the noise of the steam engine alerted Union lookouts. In both cases, the targeted vessel had time to maneuver out of the David's path—and her gunners had time to fire as well.

The Confederate navy needed some way to deliver a torpedo more effectively. Only a ship that moved silently and stealthily could accomplish the task without being detected. Two inventors in Mobile, Alabama, had created just such a

This David boat's spar, visible on the right, allowed it to deliver a torpedo directly to an enemy vessel.

secret weapon. They had built a submarine.

The idea of a submarine boat wasn't new. In the 1620s, Dutch scientist Cornelis Drebbel had built a submarine that resembled a rowboat enclosed with a leather cover. The crew rowed the vessel underwater with oars. Awkward though it was, Drebbel's submarine could remain submerged for several hours.

One hundred fifty years later, during the American Revolution, David Bushnell built the *Turtle*—the first American submarine. While the *Turtle* could navigate underwater, it failed when it tried to attack a British warship in waters off New York. In fact, no submarine had ever sunk an enemy ship. Could the men in Mobile succeed where others had failed?

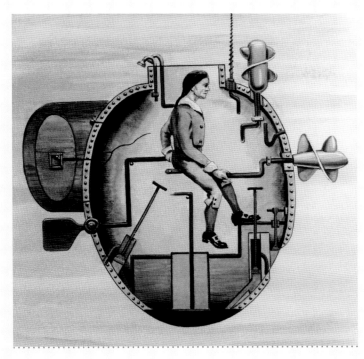

Built in 1775, the Turtle *had room for only its pilot. This 1875 drawing by Francis Barber illustrates the submarine's narrow confines.*

HORACE HUNLEY'S FISH-BOAT

Horace Lawson Hunley and James McClintock had arrived in Mobile in 1862 with high hopes. They were confident that they had solved the technical problems of past submarines and could build the blockade-busting secret weapon that the South needed. A skilled engineer, McClintock was part owner of a machine shop in New Orleans, Louisiana, where he built gauges for steam-operated equipment. His education and manufacturing experience gave him the technical expertise to build a submarine.

Horace Hunley had always dreamed of doing great things, and he had the money to make his dreams come true. The owner of a large plantation, Hunley also worked as a lawyer and a customs officer in New Orleans. The Union blockade around that city prevented him from shipping and selling his sugar and cotton crops abroad. That made him angry enough to serve as the captain of a blockade runner, a ship that moved supplies by maneuvering silently through the blockade at night.

James McClintock (LEFT) *built steam gauges and machines that made bullets before he teamed up with Horace Hunley* (RIGHT) *to investigate submarine design.*

Hunley wasn't motivated by profit alone. He believed that the Southern states had been right to secede from the United States in 1861. To help the Confederate war effort, he sought routes to transport sorely needed guns and ammunition from Cuba. He also invested thousands of dollars in submarine technology.

With Hunley's money and McClintock's expertise, the partners built two submarines in the early years of the war. Their first effort, the *Pioneer,* was very slow. When Union forces overtook New Orleans in 1862, Hunley and McClintock—fearing that she would be captured by fast Union warships—scuttled her. The inventors moved their operation to Mobile, where they built their second submarine, the *American Diver.* A rough wave swamped and sank her in Mobile Bay soon after.

Work began on the third submarine in February 1863. In recognition of Hunley's financial contributions to the building of all three vessels, the new submarine was

Despite McClintock and Hunley's efforts to protect the Pioneer *from capture, she was recovered from the seafloor by Union sailors. Fleet Engineer J. H. Shock made this drawing of what he termed the "Rebel Submarine Ram" in 1864.*

named *H. L. Hunley.* Her shape reminded many people of a fish's body, earning her the nickname "fish-boat." The *Hunley* was designed to deliver and explode a torpedo by towing it to an enemy ship. Would she live up to her inventors' hopes? The only way to find out was to test her.

Among the eager observers in that summer of 1863 was General Dabney Maury, commander of Confederate forces in Mobile. What he saw amazed him. The *Hunley* "towed a floated torpedo, dived under a ship, dragging the torpedo, which fairly exploded under the ship's bottom, and blew the fragments one hundred feet into the

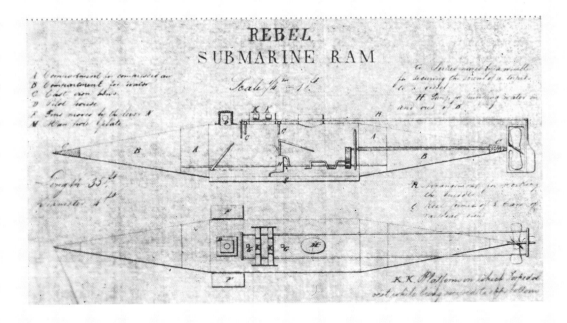

air." Unlike anchored or floating torpedoes, the *Hunley's* towed torpedo could be exploded on a specific target at a time chosen by her crew—without the noise and visibility of a David. She was everything Hunley and McClintock had dreamed of, the perfect weapon to take on the Union blockade.

The *Hunley* could do things that people had only imagined. To General Maury, her test run must have looked like magic. How could a heavy iron boat sink and then resurface? How did she cruise without sails or an engine? What made the torpedo explode on target? And how did her crew survive the experience?

Chapter Two
Climb Aboard

James McClintock was an engineer, not a magician. It was science that enabled him to create his marvelous submarine—science and hands-on experimentation. Building the Pioneer *and* American Diver *had taught McClintock a lot about what worked inside a submarine and what didn't. When he designed the* Hunley, *he corrected earlier mistakes, such as leaky seals, and added innovations, including viewing ports. Those improvements made the* Hunley *cutting-edge submarine technology.*

A sailor standing on a wharf beside the floating *Hunley* would have immediately appreciated her streamlined surface and shape. Her hull, made of iron plates, was completely smooth. The rivets that held the plates together were countersunk—set into indentations—so that their knobby heads wouldn't slow the submarine by increasing friction between the hull and the water.

The hull, almost 40 feet (12m) long, tapered to a wedge at each end. This shape was designed to channel water around the submarine, reducing friction and making it easy for the *Hunley* to glide along. The front end, or bow, had a sharp, slightly

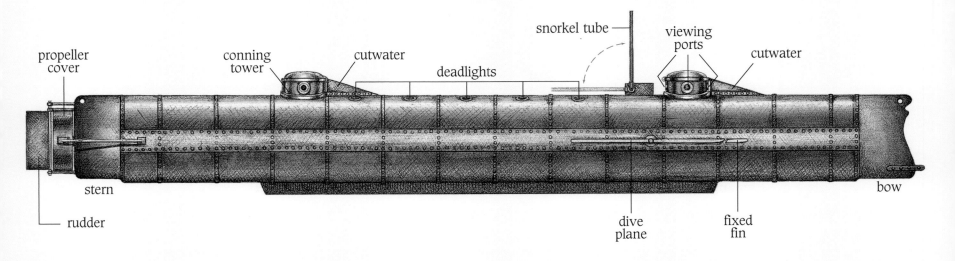

propeller cover

conning tower

cutwater

deadlights

snorkel tube

viewing ports

cutwater

stern

rudder

dive plane

fixed fin

bow

curved edge that enabled the *Hunley* to slice quietly through the water.

The stern, or back end, looked very different than the bow. A propeller with three blades was positioned here. A metal band surrounded the propeller blades. This band helped contain and direct the propeller's force, which enabled the submarine to move faster. The rudder, a flat square of metal that helped turn the *Hunley* left and right, was fastened just behind the propeller.

Two conning towers stuck up from the submarine like short chimneys. The conning towers served as entrances and exits as well as lookout stations. The word *conning* comes from the Latin word *conducere,* which means "to conduct or lead." In the forward conning tower, the captain could stand up and look out to decide where he wanted to steer the submarine. Both conning towers had thick glass viewing ports.

Each tower was streamlined in the front by a triangular piece of metal called a cutwater. The cutwaters' function was to slice through the water like a shark's fin, reducing friction and noise as the *Hunley* moved. The cutwaters also protected the conning towers from being snagged by chains or ropes dangling from targeted vessels.

A rounded hatch cover capped each conning tower. Half the crew entered through the forward hatch—the one nearest the bow—while the remainder used the aft hatch, the one nearest the stern. These narrow hatches, about 14 inches by 16 inches (35 x 40 cm) wide, were the submarine's only escape routes.

When a crewman climbed aboard, he entered a very cramped space. The crew's compartment was 4.0 feet (1.2 m) high—much too low for a man to stand in. Its width was 3.5 feet (1.1 m). Without stretching his arms to their widest, a crewman could easily touch both sides of the compartment at once.

A wooden bench fastened to the port (left) wall filled part of the compartment. Machinery took up even more space. Like McClintock's first two submarines, the *Hunley* ran on manpower. A long bar called a crankshaft ran the length of the compartment to the stern, where it connected to the propeller's shaft. Handles were positioned along the crankshaft. To move the submarine forward or backward, the crew cranked the handles, which turned the propeller. The action of the propeller's spinning blades pushed against the water and caused the submarine to move. The faster the crew cranked, the faster the *Hunley* moved.

The crank system worked well, but the bulky machinery made the interior of the submarine claustrophobic. "The propeller shaft and cranks took up so much room that it was very difficult to pass fore and aft, and when the men were in their places this was next to impossible," wrote William Alexander, a crew member and one of the engineers who had helped build the *Hunley*. The interior was dark as well as cramped. Between the conning towers, ten deadlights—circular glass ports that

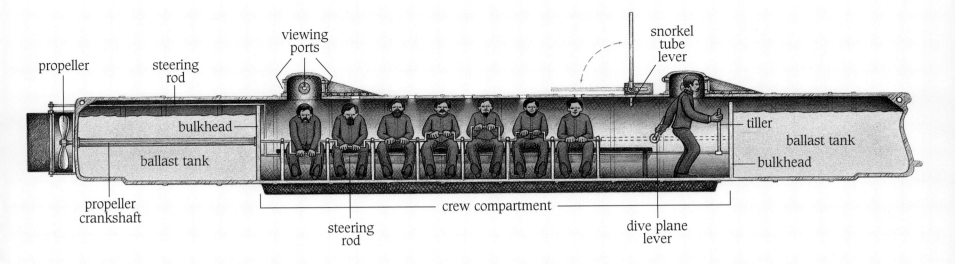

allowed sunlight to shine into the compartment—were arranged in pairs. But once the submarine dove down into the murky water, the compartment became dim. A candle was the crew's only source of light.

Cranking moved the *Hunley* back and forth, but how did she sink and rise? This was the ability that most amazed onlookers. How could an iron submarine that weighed thousands of pounds descend deep underwater and resurface? What was McClintock's secret?

DIVE!

A scientific principle called buoyancy is the key to understanding how the *Hunley*—or any submarine—is able to sink and resurface. Buoyancy starts with a simple but important scientific law: Two objects cannot be in the same space at the same time.

When a boat slides into the water, it pushes aside, or displaces, the water that is in spot.

After entering the water, the boat continues to exert force downward against the water beneath it. At the same time, the water beneath pushes upward against the vessel. The water's upward push is called a buoyant force. An object floats when the upward buoyant force is the stronger of these two forces. But the *Hunley* was made of iron, a very heavy metal. How can water hold up something so large and heavy when even a small stone sinks?

Any object will float as long as it weighs less than the weight of the water it has displaced. The *Hunley* displaced a very large amount of water that weighed more than the submarine and the air, the men, and the machinery inside her. An object that floats is said to be positively buoyant.

To make the *Hunley* sink, McClintock again relied on the principle of buoyancy.

POSITIVE BUOYANCY

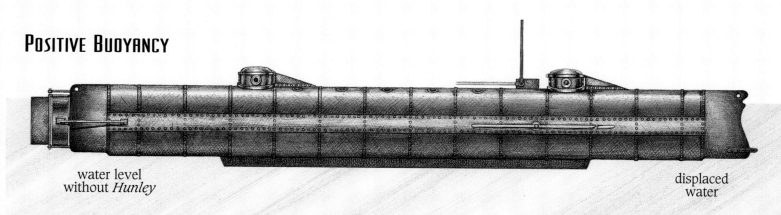

water level
without *Hunley*

displaced
water

If we could place the Hunley *in a giant swimming pool, we could observe how much water she displaces. The* Hunley *floats because she weighs less than the displaced water. She is positively buoyant.*

An object must lose some of its buoyancy to sink or dive. If an object weighs more than the water it has pushed aside, its downward force will be greater than the buoyant force. The object sinks, becoming negatively buoyant.

McClintock needed to add extra weight to make the *Hunley* submerge. But the sudden addition of a large amount of weight could have caused her to drop straight to the bottom, like a stone. To create a gradual, controllable descent, McClintock designed a long, thin flap called a dive plane for each side of the *Hunley's* hull. To dive, the captain depressed a lever that tilted the front ends of the dive planes downward. As the *Hunley* moved forward, water pressure against the slanted dive planes forced the submarine to dive gradually.

The submarine descended when the captain steadily added weight through the use of ballast. Ballast is any material—rocks, sand, metal, or even water—used to add weight to a boat. Ballast makes a floating boat more stable in the water and, in a submarine's case, easier to submerge. McClintock designed a system for the *Hunley* that allowed her to take on water as ballast, then expel it when the captain decided to rise.

To use water as ballast, the *Hunley* needed some type of tank to contain it. Both ends of the crew's compartment ended at an iron wall, or bulkhead, that was riveted to the hull. Except for 9 inches (23 cm) left open at the top, the bulkhead closed off the crew's compartment from the space that lay behind it. These two spaces, one at each end of the submarine, served as the *Hunley's* ballast tanks.

Each ballast tank had a valve called a seacock that opened to the sea. When the crew opened the seacocks, water flowed into the tanks. As the water flowed in, it pushed aside the air in the tanks. The open space at the top of each bulkhead allowed the air to be pushed into the crew's compartment. If the ballast tanks had been completely sealed off from the crew's compartment, the air would have had nowhere to go, and the water wouldn't have been able to push it aside. The air pressure inside the sealed tanks would have stopped the water from entering at all.

As water flowed into the ballast tanks, the *Hunley's* weight gradually increased. Aided by the position of the dive planes, she began to dive. It wasn't necessary to completely fill the ballast tanks to add enough weight to submerge the submarine. In fact, it would have been extremely dangerous to do so, since the top portion of each tank was open to the crew compartment. If water overflowed into the compartment, it would endanger the crew, perhaps even drown them. McClintock designed the size of the ballast tanks so that during normal operation of the submarine, water would never overflow in this manner.

The crewmen who operated the seacocks kept their eyes glued to the viewing ports in each conning tower as the water flowed in. They waited for the water level

NEGATIVE BUOYANCY

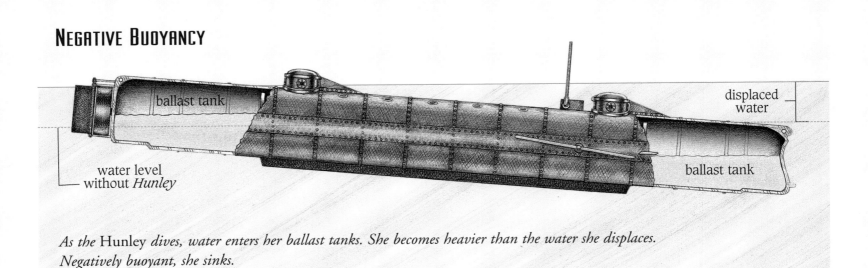

As the Hunley *dives, water enters her ballast tanks. She becomes heavier than the water she displaces. Negatively buoyant, she sinks.*

NEUTRAL BUOYANCY

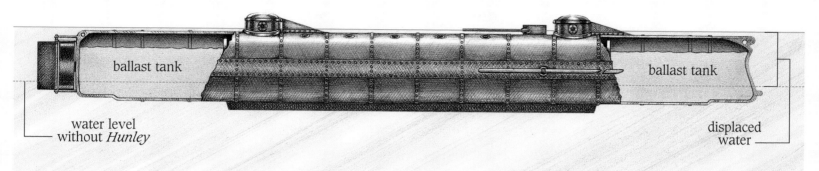

ballast tank

ballast tank

water level
without *Hunley*

displaced
water

The Hunley's *weight equals the weight of the water she displaces. She is neutrally buoyant and holds steady in the water.*

to reach a certain height on the ports. When that level was reached, they closed the seacocks, stopping the flow of water into the ballast tanks. At the same time, the captain moved the dive planes into a level position. These actions stopped the submarine from diving any deeper.

At this point, the *Hunley* had reached neutral buoyancy, a state in which her weight equaled the weight of the water she had displaced. She held steady in the water with the top of her hull about 3 inches (8 cm) beneath the surface—perfect placement for a stealth weapon that needs to remain out of sight. In this position, the submarine could cruise with her conning towers barely visible. To dive deeper so that all parts of the submarine would be submerged, the captain angled the dive planes downward as his crew cranked.

Cranking was tough, muscle-straining work. It didn't take long before the crew was breathing hard and consuming the submarine's oxygen supply rapidly. While the

Hunley was on the surface, a hatch could be opened to let in fresh air. But how did the crew get oxygen once the submarine submerged?

The crewman in the second position, just behind the captain, was responsible for bringing in fresh air. He controlled two 4.7-foot (1.4 m) iron pipes called snorkel tubes. The snorkel tubes extended from a box on the outside of the hull, just behind the forward conning tower. When not in use, the tubes lay flat against the hull. Valves inside the submarine were closed to prevent water from rushing into the tubes and flooding the crew compartment.

When the crew requested air, the second crewman swiveled the snorkel tubes upward until they were just above the water's surface, then opened the valves. He pumped a mechanism called a bellows, which sucked fresh air through the tubes into the submarine.

Safely underwater with a replenished air supply, the *Hunley* could approach her target. The captain used the viewing ports in the forward conning tower to check the location of his target. If the submarine wasn't correctly lined up with the target, the captain used a lever called a tiller to turn her. The tiller was connected to the rudder by rods that ran under the crew's bench.

As the *Hunley* approached her target, she dove and passed underneath it. Her torpedo was fastened to a wooden plank, which prevented it from sinking. The torpedo floated along the surface as it was towed behind the submarine by a 200-foot (60 m) rope. Hidden beneath the water, the submarine continued moving away from the enemy vessel until the torpedo collided with the target. The force of the collision shattered a glass vial inside the torpedo. The vial contained chemicals that cause gunpowder to ignite and explode on contact. The *Hunley's* torpedo was packed with about 90 pounds (40 kg) of gunpowder—more than enough to sink a ship.

After the torpedo exploded, the crew cranked hard and fast to a safe distance. To rise, the submarine had to lose ballast. A pump was connected to each ballast tank for this purpose. The crew pumped water out of the ballast tanks and back into the sea. As the weight of the water in the ballast tanks decreased, the *Hunley* became positively buoyant and rose.

As the crew pumped and cranked, the captain shifted the dive plane lever, this time angling the front ends of the dive planes upward. Water pressure against the dive planes made the *Hunley* rise gradually, on a diagonal path toward the surface. Once she reached the surface, the hatches could be safely opened. The exhausted crewmen welcomed the fresh air as they cranked their way homeward.

McClintock realized that in an emergency, the crew might need to rise quickly. He designed a series of detachable iron ballast weights that could be dropped from the submarine to cause a rapid weight loss. The ballast weights were fastened to the outside of the *Hunley's* keel, the central strip that runs along the bottom of a boat. The bolts that held the weights in place could be removed by the crew from inside the submarine, making her positively buoyant as quickly as possible.

As remarkable as the *Hunley* was, she did pose dangers to her crew. Because she rode low in the water, an unexpected wave could wash into an open hatch, swamping or sinking the submarine. In that event, drowning would be an all-too-real possibility. If the submarine's machinery failed during a dive, she could sink to the bottom, where the crew would soon run out of air. Those who signed on for duty were well aware of these dangers. No one could doubt the crew's courage as they attempted feats that no sailor had ever accomplished.

Chapter Three
DISASTER

With the test runs successfully completed, Horace Hunley and the submarine's other investors were eager to send her to Charleston to begin the critical mission of breaking the Union blockade. They had a financial motivation as well as a military one: A reward of $100,000 had been offered for the destruction of the USS New Ironsides or the USS Wabash, *two well-armed Union blockade ships. The reward also offered $50,000 for the destruction of a monitor, a ship covered with iron armor. If the* Hunley *sank one of these ships, her investors stood to make an enormous profit. Building the submarine had cost only $15,000.*

Shown in the foreground of this illustration, the USS New Ironsides was clad in iron armor and carried eight guns on each side. Illustration published in 1863 by Currier & Ives, artist unknown.

(No. 40.)

SPECIAL REQUISITION.

For *Nine Gray Jackets, three to be trimmed with Gold braid*

I certify that the above Requisition is correct; and that the articles specified are absolutely requisite for the public service, rendered so by the following circumstances: *that the men for whom they are ordered, are on Special Scout Service & that it is necessary that they be clothed in the Confederate Army uniform* H L Hunley

Capt G. I. Crafts A S Quartermaster, C. S. Army, will issue the articles specified in the above requisition. By *Cmd Pay Saml Rifle, Maj Estate* Aug Commanding

RECEIVED at *Charleston* the *21st* of *August* 1863 of *Capt G. I. Crafts A S* Quartermaster, C. S. Army, *The Jackets specified above*

in full of the above requisition.

(SIGNED DUPLICATES.)

H L Hunley Capt

In August 1863, Horace Hunley requested uniforms for the submarine's crew, noting that the men would be engaged in "Special Secret Service."

By mid-August 1863, James McClintock and his crew, along with the *Hunley*—lashed tightly onto two flatbed railroad cars—had arrived in Charleston. Twenty-four-year-old Emma Holmes recorded the event in her diary: "[Captain James Carlin] told us also of the *Porpoise*—the cigar-shaped boat lately arrived from Mobile. It . . . is worked by machinery & has fins like a fish, which enable it to dive. . . . It certainly is a wonderful thing, & we hope for its success." Many people mistakenly referred to the *Hunley* as the *Porpoise*. Black porpoises are a common sight in Charleston Harbor. Perhaps the *Hunley's* sleek, dark hull and porpoiselike shape gave rise to the nickname.

Although the *Hunley's* mission was urgent, James McClintock believed that the crew's safety was important too. He decided to familiarize himself and the crew with the water currents around Charleston before attempting an actual mission against an enemy vessel. He and the crew conducted a series of test dives in Charleston Harbor.

Confederate commanders, eager for action, soon grew frustrated. "The torpedo-boat has not gone out," Brigadier General Thomas L. Clingman wrote in an August

23 report. "I do not think it will render any service under its present management." In response, General Pierre G. T. Beauregard, commander of the Confederate troops in the Charleston area, removed McClintock and his crew from the *Hunley* and placed the boat under the control of the Confederate navy.

McClintock was furious. He had designed and built three remarkable submarines. He had worked more than two years perfecting his inventions and teaching the men who crewed them. With their mission close at hand, he and his well-trained group would not be allowed to see the *Hunley* go to war. McClintock doubted that a new, inexperienced crew could operate her as well.

Lieutenant John Payne, the *Hunley's* new captain, had never commanded or even served on a submarine. Yet he was confident that he and his men would succeed quickly. After just a few days of test runs, Payne believed they had mastered the *Hunley's* machinery. On August 29, he was ready to undertake a mission.

As the *Hunley* bobbed in the water near Fort Johnson, South Carolina, the Confederate steamboat *Etiwan* floated in front of her. Payne stood on top of the submarine while the crew, including Lieutenant Charles Hasker and torpedo expert Charles Sprague, settled themselves in place. Because the crew was in the process of entering the submarine, both hatches were open. What happened next has been reported in different ways.

According to Charles Hasker, Payne "got fouled in the manhole [the conning tower] by the hawser [a thick rope used to tie a ship], and in trying to clear himself got his foot on the lever which controlled the fins [dive planes]. . . . The boat made a dive while the manholes were open and she began to fill." Payne jumped off the *Hunley* as water streamed in through the forward hatch; two other crew members, including Charles Sprague, escaped through the aft hatch.

Trapped inside the submarine, Hasker clawed his way over the bar that connected the dive planes. Gasping for air, he forced his body through gushing water up into the forward conning tower. As Hasker squeezed through the hatch, the cover slammed down across his back. Frantically, he twisted and turned until only his left leg remained caught. Pressure from the surrounding water clamped the hatch cover firmly in place. Completely helpless, Hasker was "carried to the bottom in forty-two feet of water."

There he fought desperately to survive. "When the boat touched bottom I felt the pressure relax, and stooped down, took hold of the manhole plate [cover], drew out my wounded limb and swam to the surface." The five crewmen still trapped inside were not so fortunate. They all drowned.

Hasker's account places the blame for the sinking on Payne's misstep. Other accounts differ. Lieutenant C. L. Stanton, a friend and shipmate of John Payne, wrote that the accident occurred when "the line by which the [Hunley] was attached to the [Etiwan] snapped, and she went to the bottom . . . like a lump of lead." Without the addition of extra ballast, it doesn't seem possible that the Hunley could have sunk in this manner.

Yet another version of the events came from Colonel Charles Olmstead, who reported that "an unfortunate accident occurred at the wharf. . . . The submarine torpedo-boat became entangled in some way with ropes, was drawn on its side, filled, and went down." If water entered the submarine as Olmstead described, it could have added enough ballast to sink the submarine.

Regardless of what caused the Hunley to sink, the tragic deaths of the five crewmen badly shook the confidence of those who had escaped. Neither Payne nor Hasker wanted anything more to do with the *Hunley*.

General Beauregard, however, still hoped that the *Hunley* could break the Union blockade. But first, he had to get her off the bottom. The job of raising her was given to Angus Smith and David Broadfoot, two experienced deep-sea divers.

Hasker's description of the Hunley *enabled Simon Lake to make this drawing thirty-four years later, in 1897. Though several mechanical details are inaccurate, the highly claustrophobic nature of the crew's compartment is well rendered.*

Diving equipment in the 1860s was awkward and bulky. Each diver wore a cloth suit and a heavy metal helmet with a glass viewing plate. An air hose was attached to the helmet. Fresh air from the surface was pumped through the hoses to the divers as they attached chains to the submarine. Thick mud held the *Hunley* fast, but the chains, hooked to steam-powered equipment, eventually pulled her free.

The remains of the five drowned crewmen were removed from the submarine after she reached the wharf. Their bodies were buried in a Charleston cemetery, and the *Hunley* was cleaned and disinfected.

By September 14, just two weeks after she sank, the *Hunley* was ready for service again. But who would be brave enough to risk his life inside her now, especially after some people had nicknamed her the "iron coffin"? At least one person was—Horace Hunley.

The Second Crew

Horace Hunley asked General Beauregard to "place the boat in my hands" so that he could carry out the Hunley's *mission.*

Horace Hunley quickly obtained General Beauregard's permission to captain the submarine. Like James McClintock, Hunley believed that the men who built the submarine and tested her in Mobile Bay knew her best. The only crewman he chose who wasn't from Mobile was lucky Charles Sprague, who had escaped through the *Hunley's* aft hatch when she sank. Sprague was the only member of Payne's crew willing to serve on the submarine again.

The *Hunley* and her new crew took to the water like fish. Their confidence grew with each successful test dive. Before long, they would be ready to take on the Union blockade.

Early on October 15, 1863, Horace Hunley and his men gathered at Adger's Wharf. Raindrops spattered the *Hunley's* hull. Enemy vessels floating outside the harbor looked like ghost ships in the fog. Despite the nasty weather, Hunley planned several more test runs that day. With Charles Sprague and the rest of the crew, he climbed aboard the submarine. They were soon under way.

Charleston Septr 19th 1863.

General J T Beauregard.

Sir.

I am a part owner of the torpedo boat the Hunley. I have been interested in building this description of boat since the beginning of the war, and furnished the means entirely of building the predecessor of this boat which was lost in an attempt to blow up a Federal vessel off fort Morgan Mobile Harbor. I feel therefore a deep interest in its success. I propose if you will place the boat in my hands to furnish a crew (in whole or in part) from Mobile who are well acquainted with its management, & make the attempt to destroy a vessel of the enemy as early as practicable

Very Respectfully,

Your Obt. Servt,

H. L. Hunley.

The tests began with a successful dive under a friendly ship, the *Indian Chief*. The *Hunley* set out for a second dive. Immediately, something looked wrong to the observers on the *Indian Chief*. "As soon as she sank, air bubbles were seen to rise to surface of the water," a soldier recorded in the Confederate army's *Journal of Operations*. The bubbles suggested that air had rapidly escaped from within the submarine. If so, could the crew have survived the loss of oxygen? From his vantage point on the *Indian Chief*, Lieutenant Stanton—who had also witnessed the submarine's first sinking—confirmed the onlookers' fears, reporting that "when, after half an hour had elapsed, she failed to come to the surface we knew the men in her were dead."

Less than two months after her first sinking, the *Hunley* had gone down again. With her went Horace L. Hunley, the man for whom she had been named. And Charles Sprague's luck had run out. This time there were no survivors.

Chapter Four
LIEUTENANT DIXON'S MISSION

George Dixon's sweetheart, Queen Bennett, is said to have given him a twenty-dollar gold coin that saved his life.

Twenty-four-year-old Lieutenant George E. Dixon's journey to the *Hunley* was roundabout. Before the war, he had been a steamboat engineer. After the war started, he enlisted in the Twenty-First Alabama Infantry Regiment. At the Battle of Shiloh on April 6, 1862, Dixon was wounded in his left thigh, an injury that should have killed him. But the bullet struck a gold coin that Dixon was carrying—according to legend, a gift from his sweetheart, Queen Bennett.

The lucky coin saved Dixon's life. He was sent to recover in Mobile, where he met William Alexander, one of the men who had helped build and operate the *American Diver* and the *Hunley*. Dixon became part of James McClintock's submarine-building team. He often went out on test runs in the *Hunley* and, if space had permitted, would have been a member of Horace Hunley's ill-fated crew.

Although Dixon was saddened by the deaths of Horace Hunley and his crew, he hadn't lost faith in the submarine. Less than two days after the accident, Dixon and William Alexander began to talk about putting the *Hunley* back in service and forming a third crew. Dixon requested General Beauregard's permission to do so.

While Dixon awaited the general's reply, Angus Smith was diving yet again in Charleston. On October 18, he located the *Hunley*, her bow wedged deeply in the mud. The men who opened the hatches after Smith raised her found a gruesome sight. "The unfortunate men were contorted into all kinds of horrible attitudes; some clutching candles, evidently trying to force open the man-holes; others lying in the bottom tightly grappled together. . . . The blackened faces of all [caused by suffocation] presented the expression of their despair and agony," General Beauregard reported.

Appalled by the fate of Horace Hunley's crew, Beauregard sent a telegram to Dixon: "I CAN HAVE NOTHING MORE TO DO WITH THAT SUBMARINE BOAT. TIS MORE DANGEROUS TO THOSE WHO USE IT THAN TO [THE] ENEMY."

Why had the *Hunley* sunk this time? Dixon and Alexander knew that they had to solve this mystery if they hoped to convince General Beauregard that the *Hunley* was still worth taking to sea.

As the men examined the submarine, they found several clues. Horace Hunley's body was in the forward conning tower. His right hand was on top of his head, as if he'd been trying to push open the hatch. He clutched an unlit candle in his left hand. Another crewman, Thomas Park, was in the aft hatchway. It appeared that he had been trying to open that hatch too. It seemed as if the crew had attempted to escape, but the water pressure outside the submarine held both hatches tightly shut.

Dixon requested labor from enslaved men, whom he referred to as "Ten Negroes," to clean the Hunley *after its second sinking.*

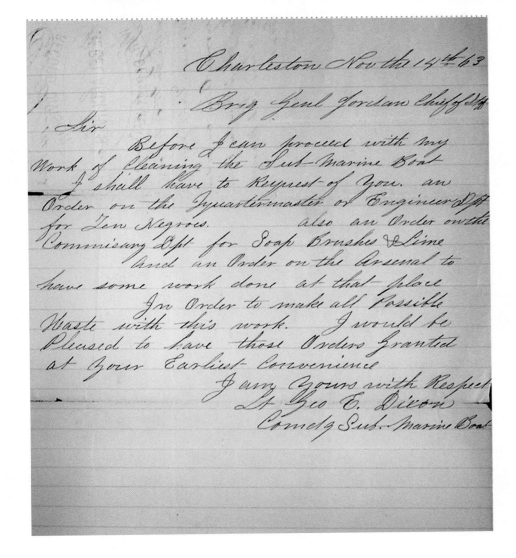

Charleston Nov the 14th 63

Brig Genl Jordan Chief of Staff

Sir

Before I can proceed with my Work of Cleaning the Sub-Marine Boat I shall have to Request of You an Order on the Quartermaster or Engineer Dpt for Ten Negroes. also an Order on the Commisary Dpt for Soap Brushes & Lime and an Order on the Arsenal to have some work done at that place In Order to make all Possible Haste with this work. I would be Pleased to have those Orders Granted at Your Earliest Convenience

I am Yours with Respect
Lt Geo E. Dixon
Comdg Sub-Marine Boat

An examination of the bolts that held the keel's iron ballast weights in place showed that they had been turned, but not enough to release the weights. This, Alexander realized, prevented the crew from dropping the ballast bars and getting a quick weight-loss boost toward positive buoyancy.

The forward seacock provided the final piece of evidence. This seacock, where Horace Hunley was stationed, was open. Water must have been rushing into the forward ballast tank even as Hunley tried to pump water out. Park's ballast tank, at the submarine's stern, had been pumped dry; his seacock was closed.

Alexander concluded that Horace Hunley had tipped the fins to dive and, in order to descend, had opened the forward seacock to add ballast. As water covered the glass viewing ports, the crew's compartment would have quickly darkened. "[Hunley] then undertook to light the candle. While trying to do this the tank quickly flooded, and under great pressure the boat sank very fast . . . and soon overflowed. . . . [The rising] water soon forced the air to the top of the boat and into the hatchways, where Captains Hunley and Park were found."

Why didn't Horace Hunley pump the water out, as Thomas Park had done at the aft ballast tank? Alexander was sure that Hunley had tried but had forgotten to close the seacock. Every bit of water that he pumped out was replaced by water flowing in.

It was clear to Alexander and Dixon that pilot error caused the tragic accident. The mystery solved, Dixon again asked Beauregard for command of the submarine. Whatever he said must have been convincing. By November 14, 1863, George Dixon was the *Hunley's* new captain.

William Alexander, about thirty-five years after serving on the Hunley

BACK IN SERVICE

Hoping to avoid another accident, General Beauregard issued a new order: No more diving to deliver a torpedo. That meant Dixon had to find another way to carry the explosive to his target. He decided refit the *Hunley* with a spar, the polelike device used on David boats. The spar would allow the submarine to ram an enemy vessel and explode the torpedo near the water's surface, without diving under the ship. The spar also gave Dixon complete control of the torpedo and its placement.

Next, Dixon searched for another crew. William Alexander would take charge of the pump and other machinery in the aft. General Beauregard allowed Dixon to ask for volunteers from the crew of the *Indian Chief* but insisted that they be told of the submarine's two accidents and the men who had drowned. Despite this warning, a number of sailors immediately volunteered. Dixon was well satisfied with them. "I have got a splendid crew of men the best I think I [have] ever seen," he wrote to a friend back in Mobile.

Dixon's crew moved the *Hunley* to a wharf on nearby Sullivan's Island and began a rigorous training schedule. Four nights a week, under cover of darkness, the *Hunley* set out on a practice mission, cruising just beneath the surface. Dixon set his course toward a targeted vessel, typically 6 to 7 miles (10–11 km) out to sea.

The crew became skilled at sneaking close to Union vessels. Alexander recalled times when they "came to the surface for air, opened the cover, and heard the men in the . . . [Union] boats talking and singing." Dixon confidently asserted that "when the night [of the mission] does come . . . I will surprise the Yankees completely."

Despite the *Hunley's* stealth, Union lookouts were a constant hazard. Because the *Hunley* was too slow to escape a steam-powered ship, Dixon believed that diving and hiding on the bottom was the best strategy to shield the submarine from enemy lookouts and gunfire. Although General Beauregard had forbidden Dixon to dive under an enemy ship while delivering a torpedo, he hadn't said the *Hunley* couldn't dive *after* doing so.

With this plan in mind, Dixon led practice dives to the bottom. Once, he and Alexander conducted a timed test to see how long they could remain submerged. "It was agreed by all hands, to sink and let the boat rest on the bottom . . . if any one in the boat felt that he must come to the surface for air, and he gave the word 'up,' we would at once bring the boat to the surface," Alexander recalled.

The test almost killed them. According to Alexander, "Dixon and myself and several of the crew compared watches . . . and sank for the test. In twenty-five minutes . . . the candle would not burn [due to lack of oxygen]. . . . " The men sat quietly and waited, no one wanting to give in first. Suddenly, all together, the crew said "up."

Immediately, Dixon and Alexander turned to their pumps. Imagine the crew's horror when Alexander's pump wouldn't work! Were they doomed to die from lack of air, as Horace Hunley and his crew had?

In darkness thicker than black paint, Alexander's fingers searched for the pump's cap. Opening it, he dug inside. Finally, his fingers grasped the problem—a piece of seaweed. In moments Alexander had the blockage cleared. With the pump working normally, the *Hunley* and her crew were soon back on the surface. To their amazement, they discovered they'd been underwater for two hours and thirty-five minutes! A soldier on the wharf told the crew that they had been reported dead.

As January 1864 drew to a close, Dixon and his crew waited for their chance to strike. For weeks sharp winds churned the seas. Although eager to carry out his mission, Dixon wouldn't take unnecessary chances with the *Hunley*. He knew that choppy seas could sink her.

Then an unexpected order left the *Hunley* short one crewman. On February 5, Alexander was commanded to return to Mobile. Bitterly disappointed, he obeyed orders and left his friends to their work. Dixon searched for a replacement.

Finally, on February 17, the winds calmed. One at a time, Dixon's crew squeezed through the *Hunley's* forward and aft hatchways. Moonlight flickered on the water's surface. Dixon had hoped that darkness would cloak the *Hunley's* mission. He willingly traded that protection for this evening's safer seas.

Shortly before 7:00, Dixon lowered himself into the dark, ice-cold submarine.

By candlelight he made a final check inside. Did they have the signal lantern? Later—if the mission succeeded—it would flash a signal to soldiers watching from shore. In response they would light a fire, a beacon to guide the *Hunley* home.

The crew was ready; the forward and aft hatches were closed and fastened. George Dixon settled himself in place and gave the order to start cranking. The mission was under way.

Artist Mort Künstler's 2003 painting The Final Mission *shows Dixon and his crew preparing to enter the* Hunley *on February 17, 1864.*

A Strange Floating Object

Landsman Robert Flemming was an African American sailor on the USS *Housatonic*, a Union steam sloop anchored a few miles from the Charleston shore. Flemming came on duty at 8:00 on the night of February 17. As a lookout, he took his job seriously. Confederate David boats were in the area, and Captain Charles Pickering had ordered the ship's fires banked, ready to make steam at a moment's notice.

At about 8:45, Flemming saw something floating about 400 feet (120 m) off the

Housatonic's starboard side, heading toward the ship. He reported the object to Lewis Cornthwait, an officer stationed nearby, who said that it was a log. Flemming pointed out that the object "was not floating with the tide as a log would, but moving across the tide." As Cornthwait examined the object with a spyglass, another officer, John Crosby, saw "something on the water, which at first looked to me like a porpoise, coming to the surface to blow." It was clear that the object wasn't a log.

Meanwhile, inside the *Hunley,* Dixon gave orders to crank faster. With adrenalin pumping through their bodies and their target within reach, his men cranked with every bit of strength they had. The *Hunley* charged toward the *Housatonic,* churning the surrounding water into small white waves. The submarine's crew braced for a crash.

On the *Housatonic,* Crosby beat the gong to call the crew to their battle stations. Captain Pickering raced from his cabin onto the deck. He and several other crewmen fired their guns at the *Hunley.* By then they knew that an enemy ship was closing in fast. There was no time for escape.

Moments later the *Hunley's* spar punched through the *Housatonic's* hull. With their torpedo planted, the crew reversed the direction of their cranking and backed

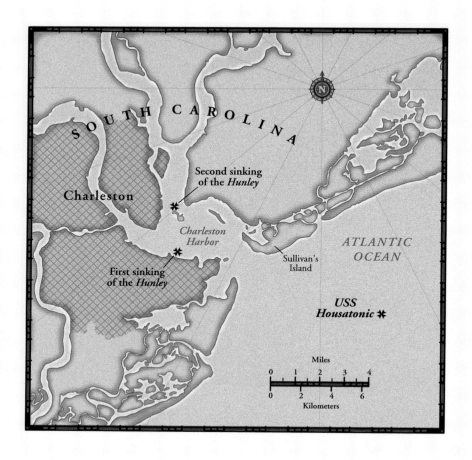

away. Dixon pulled the lanyard to trigger the explosion. A firing pin inside the torpedo ignited the gunpowder.

The torpedo exploded with a muffled noise that sounded to Robert Flemming like "wood splashing into water." Black smoke rose from the *Housatonic*. The ship's deck listed sharply to port and shuddered, as if she'd struck bottom. Then timbers cracked apart and wood flew everywhere.

The explosion threw Captain Pickering into the air. Although he was badly bruised when he landed, he was luckier than some: A few men were killed immediately. Others scrambled into the rigging, the network of ropes on the ship's masts. In the water, men swam for the lifeboats. The *Housatonic* sank rapidly, stern first. In less than five minutes, her hull hit bottom, completely submerged in 28 feet (8.5 m) of ice-cold water. Only her masts remained visible.

The USS Housatonic, *as depicted in 1902 by R. G. Skerrett*

From the rigging, Captain Pickering ordered John Crosby to row for help to the USS *Canandaigua*, anchored 2 miles (3 km) away. The *Canandaigua* quickly steamed to the rescue. By 9:35 her lifeboats were collecting survivors. One hundred fifty-eight sailors gratefully climbed aboard. Amazingly, only five men had been killed.

On Sullivan's Island, Confederate soldiers awaited the *Hunley's* return. "The signals agreed [upon] . . . to be given in case the boat wished a light . . . as a guide for its return were observed and answered," reported Lieutenant Colonel O. M. Dantzler. Having seen a light that they believed to be Dixon's signal, the soldiers lit a beacon fire in response.

Two things soon became clear. The first was that the *Hunley* had just earned her place in history as the first submarine to sink an enemy ship in war. The second was that something had gone wrong. After lighting their signal fire, the soldiers on Sullivan's Island waited for the *Hunley* to return. Several days later, they were still waiting. Was the light the soldiers had seen really made by Dixon? Or had it come from another ship, perhaps the *Canandaigua*? No one knows.

The *Hunley* never came back to port. She had gone down a third time, taking George Dixon and his men with her. Why had she sunk? What had happened to the crew? These questions went to the ocean floor with the submarine, perhaps to remain unanswered forever. After all, even if the *Hunley* and her crew were found, they couldn't talk. Or could they?

Chapter Five

A Stunning Discovery

The destruction of the Housatonic, *trumpeted in Charleston's newspaper headlines, gave the city's people hope. Yet the* Hunley's *success wasn't enough to alter the course of the sea war. The blockade remained in place around the city's harbor.*

That November Union divers searched the wreck of the *Housatonic* to see if parts of the ship could be salvaged. Union naval commanders were eager to locate the *Hunley* too. Perhaps her technology could benefit their navy. Divers dragged the area with grappling hooks and chains, but they didn't find the missing submarine.

The *Hunley* was still missing when the Civil War ended with the Union's victory in the spring of 1865. A few years later, diver Angus Smith, who had raised the *Hunley* twice before, claimed to have spotted the submarine but was unable to raise her. The murky water outside the harbor hid her well from other searchers. Over time, sand and mud buried her entirely.

As the years passed, the *Hunley* became a legend. Southerners took pride in the submarine's ingenuity and her crew's courage. P. T. Barnum, the famous circus owner, offered a $100,000 reward to anyone who could find her. William Alexander, the crewman who had been sent to Mobile before the submarine's fateful last mission, added to the *Hunley's* legacy in 1902 by publishing articles to ensure that she and her crew would be remembered and honored.

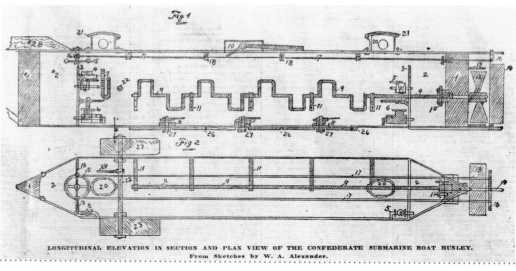

LONGITUDINAL ELEVATION IN SECTION AND PLAN VIEW OF THE CONFEDERATE SUBMARINE BOAT HUNLEY.
From Sketches by W. A. Alexander.

These 1902 drawings, based on sketches by William Alexander, show his recollections of the Hunley *as seen from the side (TOP) and from above (BOTTOM).*

The *Hunley* also took on importance as a significant artifact—a man-made object—of naval history and the Civil War era. Historians dreamed of finding the machine that had made possible a new kind of ocean warfare. They wondered how the *Hunley* worked and puzzled over what had happened to her crew.

For more than 130 years, divers kept up the search. Although several claimed to have spotted the *Hunley*, none could find the wreck again. Without evidence—a photograph or an exact location—their claims couldn't be proven.

Starting in the 1980s, Clive Cussler became one of the people most devoted to the search for the *Hunley*. An author of underwater archaeological adventure novels, Cussler is also the founder of the National Underwater and Marine Agency (NUMA), an organization dedicated to finding and preserving shipwrecks. He enjoys both the thrill of an underwater search and Civil War history. As a boy, he was intrigued by the *Hunley's* story. As an adult, he found hunting for the submarine irresistible.

Cussler and NUMA divers began their search for the submarine during the summers of 1980 and 1981. They used a magnetometer, an electronic instrument that measures the strength of the earth's magnetic field—the area where the earth's magnetic forces are exerted. A magnetometer detects any iron object as an irregularity in the earth's magnetic field. The NUMA team placed a magnetometer in the ocean and towed it behind a search boat.

Reports from the Civil War era claimed that the *Hunley* had been spotted near the wreckage of the *Housatonic*. So Cussler's team located the *Housatonic* and scanned the area around it—without success. An expanded search resulted in the discovery of several wrecks and plenty of iron scraps, but not the *Hunley*. Other work demanded Cussler's attention, and he reluctantly halted the search. But he didn't forget the Civil War submarine.

In the early 1990s, Cussler and underwater archaeologists Wes Hall and Ralph Wilbanks teamed up with archaeologists from the South Carolina Institute of Archaeology and Anthropology (SCIAA). In 1994 they used a magnetometer to identify suspect targets, iron objects that could be the *Hunley*. Harry Pecorelli III, an underwater archaeologist and one of SCIAA's divers, checked out many such targets. But none of them turned out to be the *Hunley*.

The following spring, Cussler again hired Wes Hall and Ralph Wilbanks. They decided to return to every suspect target from the previous year's failed search. They planned to identify every piece of iron in the area. With Harry Pecorelli, the men set out on May 3, 1995. Pecorelli fastened on scuba gear and splashed into the water over a suspect target about 1,000 feet (300 m) from the *Housatonic*. Hall and Wilbanks watched as he swam down out of sight.

Twenty-seven feet (8.2 m) below the surface, Pecorelli probed the sand with a pole, searching for the buried target. Three feet (1 m) down, the pole hit something hard. Pecorelli marked the spot and returned to the boat for a dredge, a vacuumlike piece of equipment used to suck up sand.

Seeing the object was impossible in the murky water. After clearing a foot-wide area, Pecorelli could feel that the surface was slightly curved and smooth, not heavily covered with barnacles or other crusty material. It felt too clean for a boat that had been underwater for more than one hundred years. Pecorelli thought that the object was probably a piece of dredging pipe used for harbor maintenance. "I don't know what it is, but it's not the *Hunley*," he told the others when he surfaced.

In keeping with their plan, Hall and Pecorelli dove again, determined to find out what the large object was. When they cleared a larger area, they discovered a shape like a tree stump protruding from the object. Then Hall felt a hinge. He knew that dredging pipes don't have hinges. But he'd seen drawings of the *Hunley*, so he also knew that each of her conning towers had a hinged hatchway.

Joined by Wilbanks, the divers dredged more sand and uncovered a complete hatchway, the snorkel box behind it, and part of a dive plane. By then there was no doubt. "We knew we had it," Pecorelli recalled.

As much as the men wanted to share their find with the world immediately, it had to remain a secret. They had to protect it from treasure hunters, who were always on the lookout for the *Hunley*. "We buried it all back up and said let's get out of here before someone sees our boat sitting here for too long," said Pecorelli.

When Clive Cussler heard the good news, he told the divers to return to the site with a video camera. Three days later, they filmed ample video evidence of the site.

No one could ever say that they hadn't found the *Hunley*.

Pecorelli thought that Hall and Wilbanks were strangely quiet on the trip back to port. "Why aren't they jumping up and down?" he wondered. Hall and Wilbanks were silent because they knew what happens when anyone finds a famous shipwreck: People fight over its ownership.

THE BATTLE FOR THE *Hunley*

That's exactly what happened. The *Hunley* became the center of a raging controversy. Who owned her? The U.S. government claimed it did because the submarine was found in government-owned waters and because after the Civil War, all property of the Confederate government became U.S. property. South Carolina argued that the *Hunley* was found off South Carolina's coast and that her final ports, Charleston and Sullivan's Island, were part of South Carolina as well. Alabama claimed ownership on the grounds that the *Hunley* was built in Mobile.

People also argued about whether the submarine should be raised. Some said that she should remain on the ocean floor as an underwater war memorial. Others, recognizing the dangers of theft and destruction by unscrupulous treasure hunters, felt that she should be brought to the surface.

Months of haggling followed. Finally, in November 1995, the various parties agreed that the U.S. government would take ownership of the *Hunley*, but she would be raised and kept in South Carolina, on display, forever. An organization called the *Hunley* Commission would oversee the recovery and care of the submarine. The

Hunley Commission and a nonprofit group called the Friends of the *Hunley* brought together a group of scientists and historians from more than thirty institutions worldwide. This team would devote their full energy to the submarine's safe recovery, excavation, and conservation.

An Undersea Challenge

The team's first task—raising the 46,700-pound (21,200 kg) submarine—required months of meticulous planning. In 1863, when Angus Smith had raised the *Hunley* twice, she was a brand-new boat. Since then she had spent more than 130 years on the ocean floor. No one could accurately judge the condition of her hull plates or the rivets that held them together. One incorrect step in the raising process could break apart the submarine or send it crashing back to the ocean floor.

As the team's archaeologists inspected the hull, they looked inside the viewing ports in the conning towers. There they found yet another reason for meticulous planning. The *Hunley* was completely filled with sediment—particles of sand, rock, and mud. Knowing that the submarine's crew had almost certainly not survived her sinking, the archaeologists theorized that this sediment may have buried the crew's remains inside the submarine. Thus the *Hunley* was very likely more than a historical artifact. She was also a war grave.

This discovery posed another significant priority for the team: to treat the remains of the crew with the care and respect due to all people whose lives are sacrificed in war. The team made a commitment to do all they could to locate the

On the lookout for artifacts, archaeologist Chris Amer sifts through shells found on the seafloor by the Hunley.

crew's remains and to restore as much as possible their humanity—the facts of their identities and lives—before giving them a proper military burial.

For the moment, though, raising the submarine would have to come first. A dive team assessed the wreck and the area around it for weeks. Led by Naval Historical Center archaeologist Robert Neyland, the team dove from a recovery ship stationed above the *Hunley*. They measured and photographed the submarine. They searched the bottom for artifacts. Then they began the slow work of dredging sediment from around and above the wreck.

Working in three-hour dive shifts, the divers dredged with hoses that sucked the sediment up to the deck of the recovery ship above, where archaeologists checked it carefully. To be certain that they wouldn't miss any artifacts, however small, they washed and sorted the sediment through three sets of screen mesh.

Meanwhile, the work continued below the surface. What was it like to be underwater by the *Hunley*? "Black," reported Claire Peachey, one of the archaeologists who worked the recovery. "While we were excavating, we created our own little environment of zero visibility." Murky clouds of dredged sediment engulfed the recovery site, essentially blinding the divers.

To ensure safety in this unusual environment, each diver was equipped with a helmet called a hard hat, rather than the masks often worn by scuba divers. The hard hat was fitted with equipment that allowed communication with the recovery ship on the surface above. As a result, the communications coordinator on the ship knew the exact position of each diver at all times. The hard hat also protected the diver's head from objects that can't be seen in zero-visibility conditions.

As the area around the submarine was dredged, archaeologists uncovered several pieces of the submarine. One discovery was the snorkel tubes that had carried fresh air down to the crew. The team also found the aft cutwater—the triangular piece that had been fastened to the hull just forward of the conning tower.

State-of-the-art hard hats provided divers with the best possible lighting, protection, and communication with other team members.

Before removing these pieces from the site, the archaeologists mapped them *in situ,* in the exact, original position and place that they were found. *In situ* mapping helps archaeologists understand how artifacts relate to one another; it's a crucial step in re-creating an accurate picture of the past. To create an *in situ* map of the *Hunley's* artifacts, archaeologists measured each object—both its size and its distance from the submarine—then drew the object's position as it lay in relation to the submarine. Later, they would analyze the positions of each artifact, hoping they would help reveal what had happened as the *Hunley* sank.

As sediment was dredged from around the forward conning tower, the archaeologists uncovered a grapefruit-sized hole. Had a gunshot from the *Housatonic* made this hole? Had the hole let in water, causing the *Hunley* to sink? For the moment, these questions had to remain unanswered. The team could only patch the hole to prevent any artifacts or sediment from falling out of the submarine during the lift.

The archaeologists continued dredging until they had uncovered the top fourth of the *Hunley's* hull. They could see that the submarine was tilted about 45 degrees toward her starboard side, with her bow buried a foot deeper than her stern. The team realized that they had to keep the *Hunley* in this position so that the sediment and the artifacts inside would remain *in situ*. If anything shifted out of place, correct interpretation of the evidence would be impossible.

Another concern was the strength of the hull. Removing the sediment surrounding it would leave it unsupported. If the rivets that held the hull plates together had weakened over time, the weight of the sediment inside the submarine could be heavy enough to break them. The hull plates would then split apart, spilling the *Hunley's* contents on the seabed. To preserve the submarine's position

Dredging revealed that the bow and other parts of the Hunley *were covered with a layer of barnacles and oyster shells that had concreted, or solidified, on the hull.*

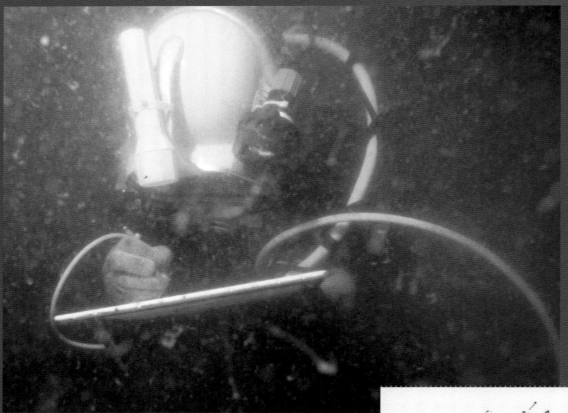

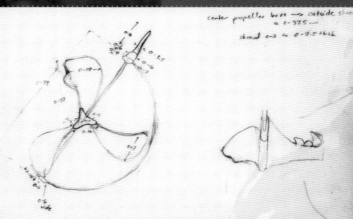

ABOVE: *Archaeologist Matt Russell uses an underwater slate to record features of the wreck site.*

RIGHT: *Careful dredging cleared the* Hunley's *propeller, sketched here on an underwater slate.*

Machinery on the divers' boat slowly lifts the spar to safety.

and keep the hull adequately supported, the archaeologists left sediment in place around the bottom three-fourths of the hull.

The team continued to adapt as they learned more about the submarine and its environment. They had hoped to raise the *Hunley* in one piece. But the surprise discovery of the torpedo spar— a piece that archaeologists had assumed had been destroyed when the *Hunley* crashed into the *Housatonic*—changed their plans. The 17-foot (5.2 m) spar was still attached to the bow of the submarine. Although the spar was intact, long exposure to seawater had weakened the metal. If left connected to the submarine, the spar would almost certainly break under the stress of the planned lift. The team had no choice but to remove the bolt that held the spar in place and lift the spar from the site separately.

RAISING THE *Hunley*

As divers worked below the surface, engineers made plans above. Since even one error could mean destruction, raising the *Hunley* would be a tricky job. The team invented a unique method to make the recovery as safe as possible. The plan called for the use of the *Karlissa B,* a specially designed barge with six legs that could be securely planted on the ocean floor to create stability. The *Karlissa B's* crane would lower a metal lifting truss—a frame of connected bars—into place around the submarine. A series of thirty-two nylon slings would be positioned under the submarine and attached to the truss for support. Finally, the crane would lift the truss and the submarine out of the water and onto a barge that would transport the *Hunley* to land.

Designing the truss and determining how many slings were needed required hundreds of mathematical calculations. "Math is a very, very powerful tool for calculating what is going to happen when you are lifting heavy yet fragile objects," noted Maria Jacobsen, the archaeologist in charge of excavating inside the *Hunley.* "You want to have your figures and understand them very accurately before you lift. It's too late to do it when you're starting the operation." The team calculated how heavy the sediment-filled submarine would be and exactly how much weight each sling needed to support.

As the recovery date approached, the crane on the *Karlissa B* lowered two 18-foot-wide (5.5 m) suction pilings, or hollow cylinders, to the seafloor. The top of each piling had been sealed to

The lifting truss, a complex frame of metal bars, was constructed on land and transported to the wreck site.

Workers prepare one of the pilings to be lowered to the seafloor.

create a solid, level platform. One piling was placed in front of the *Hunley's* bow, the other behind her stern. The open bottom of each piling settled slowly into the sand. Then engineers used suction pumps to vacuum water out of the pilings. The vacuum's force and the weight of the pilings caused them to sink deeper into the seafloor. They became stable rests for the ends of the truss.

Guided by divers in the water and the crane operator on the *Karlissa B,* the crane lowered the truss until each end rested on a piling. Starting at the bow, archaeologists excavated a trench just large enough to allow a sling to be passed under the submarine. The ends of the sling were attached to opposite sides of the truss.

As the trench near the stern was excavated, archaeologists found another surprise—the Hunley's rudder. It had broken off and lay partly under the stern. The team mapped its position *in situ,* as they had the cutwater and snorkel tubes.

After each sling was positioned, archaeologists placed a cushioning bag between the sling and the hull. The bag was inflated with soft foam that expanded to fit the shape of the hull. Within fifteen minutes, the foam set, turning into a rock-hard substance. With all thirty-two slings in place and the cushioning bags filled, the Hunley was securely nestled in her own form-fitted body cast.

How could the team know—especially in zero visibility—that the slings offered adequate support for lifting the *Hunley?* Instruments attached to the ends of each sling measured its support level. These measurements were transmitted to a computer on the *Karlissa B,* where an engineer told each diver how to adjust the sling so that its support would be exactly correct.

As the cushioning bags were placed, archaeologists uncovered two more holes. One was a pie-pan-sized opening in front of the starboard dive plane. The second was a large gash in the hull, 2 feet (0.6 m) long and about 1.5 feet (0.46 m) tall, on the starboard side near the stern. What had made these holes? Could either have been responsible for sinking the submarine? Like the smaller hole in the forward conning tower, these breaches in the hull posed questions that the team couldn't answer yet. But to ensure a safe lift, they patched the holes with foam and sheets of rigid plastic.

Recovery day—August 8, 2000—finally arrived. Five years of planning, design, and excavation had passed since Harry Pecorelli first touched the *Hunley.* On the deck of the *Karlissa B,* Jenkins Montgomery, the foreman in charge of the lift, signaled for the operation to begin. Slowly, the *Karlissa B's* crane raised the truss with the *Hunley* cradled beneath it. After 136 years on the ocean floor, the *Hunley* was about to resurface.

Sunlight strikes the Hunley *for the first time since 1864.*

The raising as seen from the air: The Titan crane lifts the truss from the water. The barge in the lower right waits to carry the Hunley to her new home.

At 8:40 in the morning, the team watched anxiously as the *Hunley* broke through the water's surface. Everyone stared as the crane positioned her above the barge that would carry her to shore. When the truss's four legs touched down safely on the deck, the team whistled, cheered, and clapped. Mission accomplished!

The *Hunley* was about to embark on a new voyage. Her destination: the Warren Lasch Conservation Center—named for the chairman of the Friends of the *Hunley*—in North Charleston, South Carolina. Her new berth would be a 90,000-gallon (340 kl) tank with a dazzling array of high-tech equipment designed to keep her safe.

The noises of roaring Jet Skis and honking horns surrounded the *Hunley* as the barge carried her to North Charleston. Above the din, Harry Pecorelli heard an even louder roar—the celebration of thousands of people lining the shore. "The cheers got louder and louder," Pecorelli recalled. "I remember thinking, oh, my gosh, you're part of something now. You're bringing the crew home."

Chapter Six
The *Hunley* Talks

As eager as the team was to begin excavating and studying the Hunley, *their first priority was to make the submarine as safe as possible. Without conservation, it would take as few as six months for the* Hunley *and many of her artifacts to deteriorate and crumble into pieces. Paul Mardikian, the team's senior conservator, leads the ongoing effort to ensure that won't happen.*

At the Warren Lasch Conservation Center, engineers lowered the *Hunley* into her tank. The water was gradually chilled to 50°F (10°C), a temperature that slows the growth of damaging fungi and algae. Keeping the *Hunley* submerged also protects her from rust, the brownish-red substance that forms when iron is exposed to oxygen and water.

The rusting process causes iron to corrode, or break down. Stabilizing the iron to stop corrosion is a crucial step in the

BELOW LEFT: *The* Hunley, *safe in the laboratory*
BELOW: *The truss and slings maintain the submarine's position at the same angle in which she was found on the seafloor.*

conservation process. Maria Jacobsen explains, "If the *Hunley* isn't stabilized, one year sitting in her tank will do more damage to her [hull and machinery] than the one hundred years she sat on the ocean bottom." To prevent such damage, a stream of electrical current, not strong enough to harm a person, runs through the water in the tank. Chemical reactions between the current and the hull halt corrosion and protect the hull from deterioration.

The tank's freshwater environment helps to shield the *Hunley* from another destructive agent—salt. During the years the submarine spent on the seafloor, salt from ocean water permeated the iron hull and machinery. Salt causes iron to deteriorate. As the *Hunley* rests in her freshwater tank, the salt leaches, or washes out, from the iron into the water. Over time, the tank's water becomes slightly salty. The tank is periodically drained, and the salty water is replaced with fresh water.

Because the *Hunley* is a complex machine with many parts held together by iron rivets, conserving her hull will require additional measures. Paul Mardikian is investigating this problem with materials scientists from around the world. Materials scientists study how and why metals and other materials break down. This part of the *Hunley* team is testing different conservation methods to determine which will be most effective in the long term. Until conservators have decided on the best methods, they will leave in place the thin layer of barnacles and young oysters that covers parts of the hull and machinery. This concretion lends protection against oxygen and other substances that cause corrosion.

With the *Hunley* safely submerged, her newest crew—archaeologists, conservators, geologists, anthropologists, and historians—spent the next six months planning the most scientifically responsible ways to reveal her secrets. Robert Neyland was insistent: He and his team wouldn't open the hull until they determined the safest way to do it. First, they needed to record as much information as possible about the submarine's exterior. This data would give scientists a baseline for later comparisons to ensure that the excavation procedures weren't causing damage.

The team began by mapping every distinctive point on the outside of the *Hunley's* hull. Archaeologists determine a point's location by measuring its position—often by hand, with a tape measure—in three directions on a baseline grid. A baseline grid is a network of lines set up across the surface of an excavation site. The grid lines cross each other like the lines on a piece of graph paper. Like a graph, an archaeological grid has one reference line called an x-axis and one called a y-axis. It also has a third axis, the z-axis, which is used to measure a feature's distance above or below the surface of the excavation—in this case, the top surface of the *Hunley's* hull.

Among the features visible in this Cyrax laser scan are, from left to right along the top of the submarine, the forward cutwater and conning tower, the snorkel box, and the aft conning tower. The propeller is also visible on the stern.

A grid is often made with plastic pipes or sometimes thin rope. The confined space within the tank and the curved shape of the hull made setting up this type of fixed physical grid extremely difficult. To solve this problem, the team marked several key points on the top surface of the hull. An instrument called a laser transit used a narrow light beam to make extremely precise measurements of these points. The measurements were then used to set up a virtual grid along the top surface of the hull.

Another problem was the sheer enormity of the mapping task. A person using a tape measure can map about three hundred points a day. Mapping the *Hunley* in this way would take years. Instead, the team used another laser, called the Cyrax laser scanning system, which can measure fifteen hundred points per *second,* even on a curved surface. And its measurements are much more accurate than those a person with a tape measure could make.

To expose the hull for scanning without compromising the truss-and-slings support, the team drained water from the tank and removed two slings from the hull at a time. The laser scanned the exposed section. Then the slings were replaced and the archaeologists moved to the next section. Within four days, the Cyrax system had recorded more than twenty million points. A computer generated a digital three-dimensional model of the submarine that is accurate to within 0.0625 inch (1.59 mm). Scientists can zoom in on specific areas of the model to study them closely.

As the archaeologists removed slings during the scanning process, they had their first opportunity to examine the hull closely in full visibility. They were eager to compare what they saw to the only detailed written description of the *Hunley,* William Alexander's 1902 articles and drawings. Other than a few letters, some sketches, and a painting from other sources, Alexander's material was the archaeologists' only reference for the submarine's design. The team had hoped that this information would guide them in planning a safe excavation.

According to Alexander, the submarine's builders had constructed her by cutting an old steam boiler in half and riveting in an additional piece of iron. The archaeologists expected a boxy, snub-nosed submarine with knobby rivets studding her hull. But Alexander's description—a forty-year-old memory at the time he recorded it—didn't match what they saw at all.

As Maria Jacobsen describes it, the *Hunley's* hull was "simply but elegantly designed." Each half of the hull—top and bottom—was made of eight iron plates. An expansion band between the two halves increased the height of the submarine. Rivets held each plate in place. Because they were countersunk, there were no knobby heads on the outside of the hull. In fact, the entire hull was as smooth as could be. But the design caused a problem for the archaeologists. How could they open the submarine without damaging the hull or the material inside?

A Grand Opening

One obvious possibility was to enter the sub just as its crew had—through the hatchways in the conning towers. Yet excavating down the narrow conning towers would be extremely awkward. Moreover, no one knew whether the hatch covers were fastened on the inside. Unfastened covers would indicate that the crew had opened or tried to open the hatches—a potentially important clue to the men's last moments and cause of death. Prying open a hatch cover to enter the submarine could destroy that information.

The archaeologists concluded that the only scientifically responsible way to open the submarine was to remove plates from the hull. Even this method caused concern. Maria Jacobsen and Paul Mardikian worried that the team might inadvertently damage machinery fastened to the inside of the hull plates—William Alexander's 1902 drawing showed rods from the rudder attached to the ceiling. Hoping to learn more, the team x-rayed the submarine, with inconclusive results. They scanned the hull with sonar, which uses sound waves to detect objects. Again they had no luck.

Philippe de Vivies removes rivets from a hull plate.

Despite the risk, the team decided to remove a U-shaped plate from the top center part of the hull. Patiently, archaeologists drilled out the ninety-four rivets that held the plate in place, a process that took ten days. Small wedges, gently tapped in around the plate's edges, loosened it from those around it.

With Alexander's drawing in mind, Jacobsen investigated further before lifting the plate. Cautiously probing for rods, she slid a thin wire between the sediment and the curved inner surface of the plate. The wire didn't snag on anything. Alexander had been wrong again: No machinery was fastened to this hull plate.

Still, the archaeologists had to be cautious. Given the likelihood that the *Hunley* was a war grave, human remains could be found anywhere within the submarine—including near the hull plate the team was about to remove. The discovery of such remains would further complicate the plate's removal because of the extra care needed to excavate them.

With preparations complete, a crane lifted the 185-pound (84 kg) hull plate. The

A crane lifts the hull plate, revealing packed sediment.

Hunley team got their first look inside the crew's compartment. They liked what they saw—a hemisphere of black sediment, molded as perfectly as a sand castle. That meant the sediment had lain undisturbed for a long time, a promising circumstance for any archaeological excavation.

Many people imagine an archaeological dig as a quest for buried objects. This is true, but the material that has buried the objects can reveal as much as the objects themselves. In the case of the *Hunley,* changing water currents had carried sediment into the submarine, where it eventually filled the hull. The team hoped that studying the sediment would help reveal two of the *Hunley's* biggest secrets—the reason why she sank and what happened to her crew.

Maria Jacobsen and Scott Harris examine the sediment's color and texture.

HIDDEN LAYERS

Stratigraphy is a branch of geology that deals with understanding how sediment layers are arranged, how they form, and what they mean. It explains the order in which layers form and the environmental conditions that existed when each layer was deposited. Scott Harris, the *Hunley* team's geologist, is an expert in this highly specialized field. He reads sediment layers like other people read the pages of a book.

To find the *Hunley's* sediment layers, the archaeologists used flat trowels to remove measured levels of sediment, always on the lookout for changes in the sediment's color or texture. Both are common features that distinguish layers. The pitch-black sediment didn't appear to have many layers, but the team felt certain that they were there. They

decided to x-ray a sediment core—a plug of material several inches thick. Because some sediment particles, such as shell and bone, absorb x-rays, they show up as bright areas on an x-ray image, just as a person's bones do. Other particles, such as certain very fine sands and clays, appear as dark areas, much as a person's organs and soft tissue do. The scientists hoped that the particles in the sediment core would respond to the x-ray in a way that would make the layers visible.

The team was right. The x-ray produced "beautiful stratigraphy, very clear [layers]," according to Maria Jacobsen. But a regular x ray creates only a flat image; it doesn't show depth. For example, a metal ball and a coin present a similar image—just a flat circle. The core x-ray couldn't show the thickness of a layer or other aspects of its shape. To interpret the stratigraphy accurately, Scott Harris needed more information.

The team removed sediment in measured levels, carefully documenting each change.

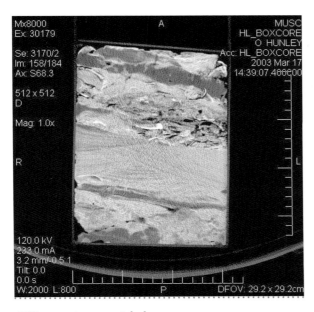

Mx8000
Ex: 30179

Se: 3170/2
Im: 158/184
Ax: S68.3

512 x 512
D

Mag: 1.0x

R

120.0 kV
233.0 mA
3.2 mm/-0.5:1
Tilt: 0.0
0.0 s
W:2000 L:800

A

MUSC
HL_BOXCORE
O HUNLEY
Acc: HL_BOXCORE
2003 Mar 17
14:39:07.466€00

L

P

DFOV: 29.2 x 29.2cm

CT scanning provided detailed data about the sediment layers, such as the coarse particles on the center right of this scan.

The team decided to perform an ultrasensitive x-ray scan called a computerized tomography (CT) scan on the core. Sometimes referred to as a CAT scan, a CT scan is the same type of scan used in medical testing for tumors and other conditions. Instead of making one image of a sediment core, as a regular x-ray machine does, a CT scanner makes many such images, called slices.

The CT scanner digitally imaged the sediment core every 0.08 to 0.12 inches (2–3 mm) and from many different angles to show the position and shape of each sediment and shell layer, as well as any other material in the core. As the submarine excavation continued, the team made CT scans of cores from all areas inside the *Hunley.* These scans gave Harris the information he needed to begin his analysis.

STRATIGRAPHY STORIES

One of the key rules of stratigraphy is that in any series of sediment layers, the top layers are deposited after the bottom layers. In the case of the *Hunley,* the sediment layers that were exposed when the top hull plates were removed were the newest. Even though these layers must have been deposited long after the *Hunley* sank, Harris knew that they might give clues to the condition of the submarine at different times in its long life on the ocean floor. These clues might help him eliminate certain possible causes of the sinking. They could also provide information about the fate of the crew and their remains.

The sediment in the top layers was soft and muddy, with some gritty sand. Harris saw winding patterns—animal burrows—in some of the CT scans. And archaeologists had found some small fish bones. Fish and burrowing creatures such as crabs, snails, and mollusks need oxygen to survive. The presence of burrows and fish bones meant that water containing at least some oxygen had deposited these sediment layers.

Harris also used a second rule of stratigraphy: Layers containing very fine particles are deposited by relatively slow-moving water. A slow-moving current contains enough energy to carry only small, light particles. The particles settle when the slow current slows further or stops. (A faster current would have enough energy to keep the particles moving.) Because the top layers contained fine mud particles and tiny sand grains, Harris concluded that the environment inside the submarine when they were deposited—possibly years after the submarine sank—was fairly calm. No large creatures or swift currents had greatly disturbed the sediment or any artifacts or human remains it contained.

The lifting of additional hull plates gave access to sediment in other parts of the submarine.

But the interior of the *Hunley* hadn't always been calm, as Harris discovered when the archaeologists troweled deeper and found a different kind of sediment. This sediment wasn't muddy. It consisted of coarse sand and broken shells. Only fast-moving water has enough energy to move heavier particles such as these. The coarse sediment layer also contained another important clue—ripple marks. These ridges are formed when water currents move back and forth regularly over sediment.

Harris concluded that the environment inside the submarine was very dynamic, or full of energy, when the coarse layer was deposited. Fast currents had swept through the *Hunley* at that time. Remembering the gash in the stern and the hole near the dive plane, Harris observed that these breaches in the hull must have allowed swift currents into the submarine. Could either the gash or the hole have been made when the *Hunley* crashed into the *Housatonic?* Had either caused the submarine to sink?

Harris answered these questions by looking beneath the coarse layer, where he found the first layers that had settled in the submarine. Unlike some of the layers above them, they had no burrows or other evidence of animal life. They contained slippery, blue-gray and black clay with particles even finer than those in mud. Clay particles are so light that even a very slow current keeps them moving; they settle only in very still water. That meant that these layers couldn't have formed if the *Hunley* had any large holes when she landed on the ocean floor. Water flowing swiftly through large holes would have swept away the clay particles. Harris concluded that the environment inside the *Hunley* when she first settled on the seafloor was calm and still, not dynamic at all.

Harris's stratigraphy interpretation solved one of the investigation's most significant mysteries: Did the large breaches in the hull cause the *Hunley* to sink? The answer was no. If the large holes had been made before the sinking, the bottom sediment layers would have shown evidence of dynamic water movement—coarse shells, abundant sand, and marine animals. Clearly, the holes were made sometime after the submarine sank, perhaps by the anchors of passing ships or by searchers' grappling hooks.

If there were no large holes in the hull when the *Hunley* sank, how did the bottom layers of sediment get inside? Slow-moving water and fine sediment particles may have first flowed into the *Hunley* through tiny holes, much smaller than the head of a pin, in the hull. Any water-going vessel, when submerged for a lengthy period of time, will develop small leaks. These holes would have been large enough for very fine sediment to pass through.

RUSTY SLIME

As the team removed more sediment, they discovered another geological mystery on the inside of the hull—intriguing formations called rusticles. Rusticles resemble icicles in shape and can form in different ways. The *Hunley's* rusticles formed when microorganisms chemically reacted with the iron hull. The result was a thick, rusty slime that flowed downward along the inside of the hull, the way paint that's applied too thickly flows down a wall. When the flow reached a ridge on the hull, it stopped, forming a drip. Over time, new drips accumulated on top of older drips. Eventually, the drips solidified, forming rusticles.

Some *Hunley* observers suggested that the presence of rusticles indicated that water didn't enter the submarine for many years. How could the rusty slime have formed drips that had time to solidify in an environment filled with water? Wouldn't the water have washed them away? But if the submarine wasn't flooded, why did she sink? And what happened to her crew?

One possibility is that Dixon may have intentionally descended to hide or to allow the crew to rest at the bottom after sinking the *Housatonic*. Thus the *Hunley* would have been safely airtight when she reached the seafloor. At that point, a mechanical malfunction could have kept the crew from ascending. Or, if the men rested too long and the compartment began to run out of oxygen, they may have become dizzy and lost consciousness. In either case, the men would have suffocated within hours of reaching the bottom. The drips would have then formed in the water-free submarine.

According to Scott Harris, though, the geological evidence doesn't prove this theory to be true. Rusticles don't have to form in an air-filled space. Because the slimy material that creates them is heavier than water, it can form drips that are just heavy enough that still or slowly moving water doesn't wash them away. Future laboratory analysis may help Harris to determine exactly when and how the *Hunley's* rusticles formed.

Harris's studies provided some important information about what had happened inside the *Hunley* as she lay on the seafloor. But many puzzles remained for Maria Jacobsen and her team of archaeologists to solve as they continued to excavate the submarine.

Chapter Seven
BURIED TREASURES

As Scott Harris studied the Hunley's *stratigraphy*, the archaeologists labored under challenging, often unpleasant conditions. Everything inside and outside the submarine had to be kept wet at all times to maintain the hull's stability and to prevent the drying out of any artifacts or human remains under the sediment, which would cause deterioration. For these reasons, the tank's water level was lowered only enough to expose the areas being excavated. Hoses continually sprayed those areas with water. During the early stages of the excavation, the archaeologists often stooped, sat, or lay in cold water.

At the best of times, the team's work space was cramped. For parts of the excavation, the archaeologists dug into the exposed sediment while lying on boards suspended outside the submarine. As the work progressed, more hull plates were removed, and the scientists were able to enter the submarine. They knelt and lay on wood and rigid plastic sheets as they worked. This scaffolding supported the scientists' weight and protected any fragile artifacts that might be buried below. Eventually, the team squatted in cleared spaces throughout the submarine.

BELOW LEFT: *Harry Pecorelli excavates a narrow trench within the submarine's interior.* BELOW: *John Dangerfield uses a stream of water to push sediment through a series of screens.*

The air quality inside the *Hunley* was terrible. The rotten-egg smell caused by decaying marine life made breathing difficult. "The air was very foul [in certain areas]. . . . We had to rig up an air ventilation system [to carry in fresh air] to allow work to continue," recalled Maria Jacobsen.

At first, the team found nothing but sediment and more sediment. As this material was removed from the submarine, it was sifted through a series of mesh screens, just as the sediment that surrounded the *Hunley* on the seafloor had been. The sifting ensured that even the tiniest artifacts or fragments of human remains wouldn't be overlooked.

Although the archaeologists didn't uncover any artifacts in the first days of the excavation, they did discover why the hull x-rays they'd taken earlier hadn't revealed any useful data. The sediment was so tightly packed that the x-rays couldn't penetrate it.

After days of painstaking trowel work, archaeologist Shea McLean was thrilled to discover the first loose artifact of the dig.

This curious round object was covered with so much concretion that the archaeologists couldn't determine whether it was made of wood or metal. It had horizontal slats that looked as though they might have opened and closed. What could it be? Further excavation revealed the answer: Identical objects covered the deadlights, the glass ports that allowed light into the crew's compartment. Why would the deadlights need covers? The archaeologists realized that candlelight shining through the deadlights would have revealed the *Hunley's* position to the enemy. James McClintock had taken care of that problem with the first submarine window blinds!

MAP, MAP, MAP

No matter how eager the archaeologists were to see what they would find next, before moving on, they had to map every artifact and feature they encountered *in situ*. But the Cyrax laser scanning system, perfect for rapidly mapping the exterior, cannot be used in water. Moreover, it was too bulky to function in the cramped, closed environment of the submarine's interior.

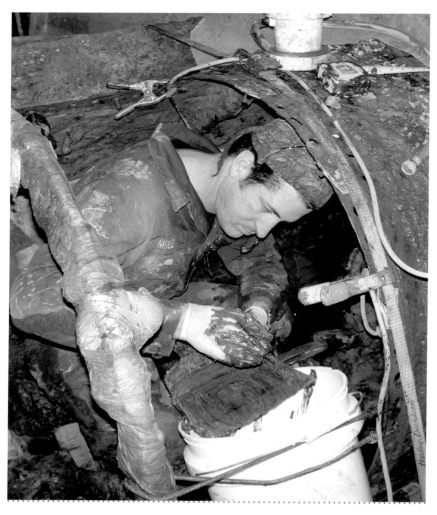

Shea McLean squats in the crew's compartment as he searches for artifacts.

Instead, the *Hunley* archaeologists opted to use the Vulcan 3D Measurement System. This digital system features two spinning laser transmitters. From their positions on the truss, the transmitters sent laser beams across the entire field of the *Hunley's* tank. To measure and record an artifact's position, archaeologists used an electrical sensing wand with a light receiver on the tip. The tip was placed by the artifact. As the laser beams from the transmitters hit the light receiver, it measured the artifact's position based on the angles of the beams.

Harry Pecorelli uses the Vulcan 3D Measurement System as Maria Jacobsen assists from within the Hunley.

The resulting data was instantly transmitted to a handheld computer attached to the wand, which continuously calculated the position of the receiver and the artifact. All the data collected in this manner can be incorporated into the Cyrax system. Eventually, the team will make a three-dimensional map of the interior of the Hunley that shows the positions of all the artifacts and machinery.

PRESERVING THE PAST

As the excavation continued, the archaeologists began to find items that had belonged to the crew: buttons, hats, part of a leather belt, a leather wallet, two pocketknives, three pencils, four tobacco pipes, a small stoppered medicine bottle with liquid inside, eight canteens, and a candle. As each item was discovered it was mapped, described in writing, sketched, photographed, and labeled with an identification number.

Further troweling revealed features of the submarine's interior. Five weeks into the excavation, the crank handles that the crew had sweated over were exposed. Shea McLean carefully uncovered the bellows, the device used to suck fresh air down through the snorkel tubes and into the submarine. Each feature and artifact reminded the archaeologists of the men who had used them.

After mapping an artifact's location, the team removed it from the submarine. Some artifacts, such as a lantern that McLean found, were too fragile to immediately remove from the sediment surrounding them. Archaeologists brought out these artifacts in block lifts, meaning that the artifact and the sediment were removed together as a block. More than forty blocks were lifted from the *Hunley*.

Every artifact was taken to the conservation laboratory for cleaning, study, and preservation. Why is the conservation of, for example, a crewman's shirt button so

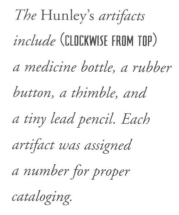

The Hunley's *artifacts include* (CLOCKWISE FROM TOP) *a medicine bottle, a rubber button, a thimble, and a tiny lead pencil. Each artifact was assigned a number for proper cataloging.*

important? Many artifacts have survived the Civil War era, but those from the *Hunley* are unique. They're significant to the history of not only the Civil War, but also submarine development and naval warfare. They're also part of a human story treasured by many people. Finally, even the smallest artifact could provide a clue to the *Hunley's* mysteries. Each must be studied and preserved for future viewing.

In the conservation lab, loose artifacts and sediment blocks were photographed and x-rayed to record their dimensions and shape. Sediment could be safely removed from hard, stable artifacts, such as a knife or a button, through careful brushing or scraping. But these methods would harm delicate artifacts or those with soft surfaces that could be easily chipped. Conservators removed the sediment from such items— a pencil, for example—with a thin stream of running water.

An instrument called a stereomicroscope, which magnifies an object up to 160 times its size, allowed the conservators to see details as they cleaned each artifact. The magnification made it easier to distinguish the artifact's surface from the sediment, preventing accidental scraping. The stereomicroscope also revealed tiny cracks and other damage, which helped the team determine how to best conserve the artifact. For even

BELOW: *All artifacts, including the lantern shown here, were x-rayed to create a record of their dimensions.*

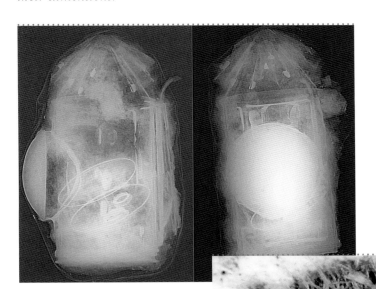

RIGHT: *Microscopic study revealed the letters* END *stamped on a fragment of fabric. The meaning of these letters is still being investigated.*

LEFT: *As the team removed more sediment, the* Hunley's *interior features emerged. Shea McLean works on one of the handles used to crank the submarine.*

BELOW: *The crew's bench can be seen on the right side of this photograph. The bench's angle is a result of the tilted position of the submarine.*

ABOVE: *When the team found a broken depth gauge containing mercury, they realized that the surrounding sediment might be contaminated with this poisonous substance. Archaeologists periodically checked the mercury level to ensure that conditions were safe for the excavation to continue.*

more minute examination, conservators used a compound microscope, which magnifies objects up to 1,000 times. The high level of magnification enabled scientists to identify cloth fibers, for example, to determine how the crew was dressed.

Many artifacts had to be examined with particular care. Over the years, the cells of organic artifacts—animal-based or plant-based materials such as leather and wood—had absorbed a great deal of water. If these artifacts were allowed to dry, the cells would lose the structural support provided by the water. The cells would collapse, and the artifact would crumble. Like the submarine itself, the organic artifacts were constantly misted with water while being examined.

Ebba Samuelsson sprays a crewman's shoe to remove sediment without damaging the leather.

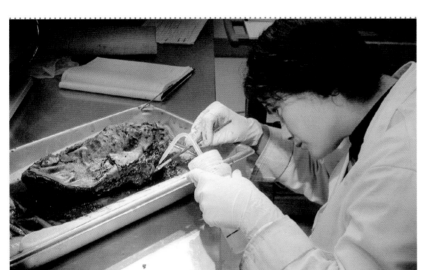

After cleaning and microscopic study, the next step was to stabilize each artifact to prevent further deterioration. Different materials require different methods of stabilization. For example, organic artifacts—a belt, a wallet, canteens—were stored in containers of water in a large walk-in refrigerated compartment. The compartment would also serve as a morgue to hold human remains after their excavation. The cold air and water, like the cold water in the submarine's tank, prevent microorganisms from destroying the material.

But stabilizing an artifact for long-term conservation requires the removal of water. Conservators safely removed water from waterlogged artifacts made of leather, wood, and certain fabrics by freeze-drying them. Each artifact was submerged in a water bath that contained a chemical called polyethylene glycol. The chemical seeped into the artifact's cells, where it provided support for the fragile cells during the f reeze-drying process. Without polyethylene glycol, the abrupt removal of water could cause the artifact's cells to collapse. That would destroy the artifact.

Next, the artifact was placed in a freeze-drying chamber. As the water froze, it changed into ice crystals. At -22°F (-30°C), the cold was so intense that the ice crystals sublimated, changing directly from ice into water vapor. A vacuum attached to the chamber gently sucked away the water vapor. When the process was completed, the water-free artifact was slowly returned to room temperature.

After being stabilized, most of the artifacts were stored in the conservation laboratory. Once the cleaning and preservation processes are complete for all of the artifacts—which will take several years—many will be put on display in the museum that will be built for the *Hunley,* where people can see for themselves the objects owned and used by the submarine's final crew.

Chapter Eight
In Touch with the Past

Throughout the excavation, the archaeologists had expected to eventually unearth the crew's remains. The first bones found were the right and left femurs, or thigh bones, of one crewman. The next day, Maria Jacobsen began to excavate the sediment that surrounded the snorkel box. This sediment was at a high level inside the submarine, about 1 foot (30 cm) beneath the hull's inner surface. Here she encountered a human rib bone. This find was followed by more rib bones, some vertebrae, and an upper arm bone.

It surprised Jacobsen to find bones so near the ceiling of the submarine. What were they doing there? The team theorized that perhaps this crewman's body had floated vup to the snorkel box, where it became entangled with the bellows. Over time, as the body's tissues decomposed, many of the crewman's bones would have sunk to the bottom of the submarine. Those entangled in the bellows would have stayed in place, where Jacobsen found them.

Later, about 1 foot (30 cm) from the bottom of the submarine, amongst artifacts and machinery, the archaeologists found more human rib bones. Many more bones followed. Foot bones were found still inside shoes that had become concreted to the hull. Other bones had rested against the crank handles and fused to them over time.

The position of these bones showed that the men in the middle part of the submarine were apparently unable to rise from the bench and move away from their stations when disaster struck the *Hunley.* Even after death, some of the men's bodies had been held in place by the crank handles.

Then came the first skull. "That was one of those moments when it became really personal," Harry Pecorelli recalled. "I was working, bent over this sediment and these guys, ten or twelve hours a day. All of a sudden, I'm looking at eye sockets. We found one skull, then another. Soon there were four or five skulls within view while we were working, looking at us the whole time."

As Shea McLean excavated the base of a skull found near the seventh crank, he uncovered a puzzling artifact—a copper identification tag belonging to someone named Ezra Chamberlin. Strangely, the tag indicated that Chamberlin was a soldier in the Seventh Regiment of Connecticut Volunteers— a Union regiment! Had a Union spy been on board the *Hunley?* Determined to find the answer, the team pursued leads in libraries, archives, and cemeteries.

Although every bone from each crewman's body was eventually located inside the submarine, none of the men's remains were found as a complete skeleton. As the tissues and ligaments that held the bones together decomposed, the skeletons had fallen apart. Bones landed in different places.

How did the identification tag of a Union soldier from Connecticut find its way into the Hunley?

Some bones became commingled, or mixed together, with those from other skeletons on the bottom of the submarine.

All human remains were mapped *in situ* when they were found. Their positions would be analyzed for information about the crew's final moments and what happened after their deaths. Next, the team removed the bones, a task that required a delicate touch and the utmost care. At times, the archaeologists abandoned their trowels and used wooden tongue depressors to excavate around the remains. No one wanted to nick a bone with a hard metal tool. After removal from the submarine, the remains were carefully stored in water inside the laboratory's refrigerator.

Upon studying the crewmen's skulls, scientists discovered that, amazingly, all of them still contained brain matter. Some bones still contained marrow. Hairs—even eyelashes—were found when the sediment that surrounded the remains was sifted. Such complete preservation of human remains is highly unusual when a body has been underwater for such a long time. In most such cases, marine organisms consume and destroy the remains within a few months or even weeks. But as Scott Harris concluded when he observed the absence of animal burrows in the *Hunley's* bottommost sediment layers, the submarine's interior environment lacked oxygen. Oxygen-breathing organisms such as crabs or fishes couldn't survive there.

Of course, there must have been some oxygen within the *Hunley* immediately after she sank. But this oxygen would have been quickly used up by bacteria and other microorganisms as the crew's bodies decomposed. The oxygen supply couldn't have been replenished until large holes were created in the hull, allowing oxygen-rich currents to flow into the submarine. In a roundabout way, by robbing the oxygen from the interior of the submarine, the crew's decaying tissues saved and preserved many of the artifacts found inside—including their own remains.

The last remains to be removed from the submarine were found beneath the forward conning tower. Since this was the position that the captain occupied, archaeologists felt sure that this man was Lieutenant George Dixon.

By this point, the team had realized that the number of crewmen was fewer than they had expected. William Alexander and other observers had noted that nine crewmen served on the submarine and that it had eight crank handles. (The captain served as the ninth crew member; he didn't operate a crank handle.) The archaeologists found only seven crank handles and eight crewmen. Either the *Hunley* had been modified or Alexander and the others had been wrong.

LOCATION OF SELECTED ARTIFACTS AND HUMAN REMAINS

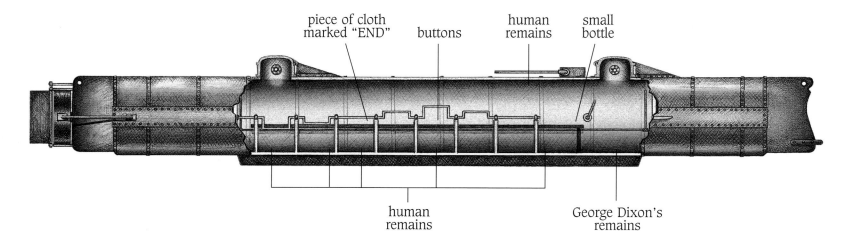

piece of cloth marked "END"　　buttons　　human remains　　small bottle

human remains

George Dixon's remains

Dixon's remains differed from those of the other crewmen. Some of his bones were articulated—still connected together as they were when Dixon was alive. For the bones to have been preserved in this way, layers of sediment must have buried Dixon's body fairly quickly, before his tissues decayed. While excavating the forward conning tower, the team determined that the hatch above Dixon's remains was not locked down. This fact, combined with stratigraphic analysis, suggested that the sediment that encased Dixon's body may have entered the submarine between the hatch cover and its rubber seal.

Cloth too fragile to touch surrounded Dixon's bones. As chief conservator, Paul Mardikian was particularly concerned that the cloth not be damaged. He and Maria Jacobsen decided that the safest way to remove Dixon's remains was in a block lift. The block of sediment would protect the cloth, the bones, and any secrets they might reveal.

DIXON'S MESSAGE

Few things excite archaeologists more than making connections with people who lived in the past. Before the *Hunley* was raised from the seafloor, Maria Jacobsen had said, "I would love to find something with somebody's name on it. That would be fantastic!" But as Jacobsen knew, paper disintegrates rapidly in water. A handwritten note from the past couldn't possibly be found in this excavation—or so she thought.

On the night of May 23, 2001, Jacobsen positioned herself alongside George Dixon's mud-encased remains, ready to begin the block lift. Outside the submarine, several team members observed the process, wondering what the block lift might contain. Earlier they had talked about the legend of Dixon's good-luck token. According to oral tradition, Dixon had always carried with him the twenty-dollar gold coin that had saved his life. Would Jacobsen find it among Dixon's remains?

The first step of the block lift was to slide a thin metal sheet beneath part of Dixon's body. To protect the remains from being scraped, Jacobsen placed her hand between the sheet and the body. Suddenly, the tip of her finger struck something thin and hard. Jacobsen knew from the object's position that it couldn't be a bone. She ran her finger along the object and immediately realized that it was a coin—a big one, just where Dixon's left trouser pocket would have been.

Even before she rinsed away the sediment, Jacobsen could feel that the coin was bent as though it had been warped by a strong impact. Sitting in the submarine, wet up to her neck, Maria Jacobsen knew that she held the coin that had saved Dixon's life at the Battle of Shiloh, a token so important to him that he had carried it on his last mission. As the other team members yelled with excitement, Jacobsen flipped the coin over. There, on the back, was an inscription no one had known existed:

Maria Jacobsen examines the coin found with Dixon's remains.

Dixon's twenty-dollar gold
piece was minted in 1860,
before the Civil War began.

"This was my dream come true," Jacobsen remembered. "It's a note, but how elegant—a note written on a gold coin. Finding that inscription and holding that coin was one of the most powerful experiences I've ever had. It was a real touch with the past and a real message, something that comes once in a lifetime."

MORE SURPRISES

After this astonishing discovery, the team looked forward to examining the seven sediment blocks that contained Dixon's remains. Jacobsen and Mardikian knew that excavating the sediment around Dixon's clothes and remains would be particularly difficult. The waterlogged fibers of his garments were so fragile that the slightest touch could dislodge fragments and destroy the cloth.

To solve this problem, the *Hunley* scientists invented a new excavation technique. They began with a CT scan of one of the blocks. The scan revealed the positions of the sediment, the cloth, and a pocket watch attached to a chain. The scan showed the scientists exactly how each item related to those around it.

Next, the team placed the block in a basin of water on a platform. To remove the sediment surrounding the cloth, they filled a syringe with water. Pushing the plunger created a gentle water current across the block. As tiny bits of sediment floated from the block, the scientists vacuumed them away with a catheter, a flexible tube thinner than the lead in a pencil.

"Slowly, slowly, we exposed the cloth and documented it," recalled Maria Jacobsen. "Because the fibers remained suspended in water, they didn't have to carry weight." Throughout the excavation, the water continuously supported the cloth and kept it from crumbing under its own weight.

The steady removal of the cloth and sediment uncovered the pocket watch, revealing that it was made of gold. When the watch was opened, the team discovered that although the minute hand and second hand were well preserved, two-thirds of the hour hand had broken off. But after the interior of the watch was cleaned, watch experts were able to determine that it had stopped at 8:23—near the time of night that Robert Flemming and other *Housatonic* crewmen reported being hit by the *Hunley.*

The watch could provide important clues about the circumstances of the crew's death. This type of watch cannot operate underwater. If the *Hunley* sank and flooded shortly after she attacked the *Housatonic,* the water would have stopped the watch at

The team conducted seven block lifts to remove Dixon's remains as safely as possible.

that time. If this was the case, the crew must have drowned at that time as well.

But this type of watch also requires periodic rewinding to continue to operate. Is it possible that the watch simply ran down—for example, at 8:23 the next morning—because it hadn't been rewound? For the watch to stop this way, it would have to have been in a waterless environment. This possibility supports the theory that the crew may have died by suffocation rather than by drowning.

The *Hunley* team is working with watch experts to determine what caused the watch to stop. If this analysis yields conclusive results, the mystery of what caused the death of the crewmen may be solved—and this may, in turn, help explain how the submarine came to rest on the seafloor.

Dixon's pocket watch and a diamond brooch found during the excavation of his remains suggest that he may have been wealthy.

Chapter Nine
FORENSIC TALES

"Bringing the people back is what archaeology is all about," says Harry Pecorelli. By the summer of 2001, Pecorelli and the other team archaeologists had excavated more than 1,600 human bones from the Hunley. As some members of the team focused on artifact conservation and unraveling the mystery of how the Hunley sank, others brought their talents to bear on restoring the crew's humanity—identifying the remains and learning as much as possible about the men's lives.

No complete, reliable list of the crew's names and ages existed. Many official Confederate records were destroyed in the war's final days so that Union troops couldn't capture them. It would take an experienced researcher to interpret the scattered evidence that had survived the war.

Linda Abrams, the team's forensic genealogist, specializes in tracking down people who have been lost in history. How does she learn about the lives of those who have been dead for decades—or, in the case of the Hunley's crew, much longer? "I try to find a paper trail," she explained, "the written records people leave of their lives."

Abrams began her search with William Alexander's articles, a letter he wrote in 1898, and a few historical documents written by other people. These materials proffered eight names: George E. Dixon, James A. Wicks, Arnold Becker, Fred or Frank Collins, C. Simpkins, Joseph Ridgeway, C. F. Carlson, and Miller, whose first name couldn't be determined.

Abrams's search for information about the crew took her to more than ten states. She read thousands of historical documents, such as military, marriage, and census records, searching for the names of the *Hunley* crewmen. She interviewed the staff members of state archives, historical societies, libraries, and courthouses.

The research was made more difficult by spelling irregularities in the crewmen's names. Three names—Ridgeway, Carlson, and Simpkins—were spelled several different ways. For her official record, whenever possible, Abrams chose the spelling a crewman had used when signing his own name. Thus these names were officially recorded as Ridgaway, J. F. Carlsen, and Lumpkin.

Despite the challenges, Abrams uncovered a great deal of information. A crewman named James Wicks, she learned, was married and the father of four daughters. Before the war, George Dixon had worked as a riverboat engineer. Frank Collins had been raised in his grandparents' home in Virginia. J. F. Carlsen had served aboard a blockade runner.

As Abrams worked to discover the details of the men's lives, the team's archaeologists studied their remains. The first step was to sort the bones into individual skeletons. Except for a few finger bones that were concreted to the hull, the archaeologists felt certain that each crew member's skeleton could be completely reassembled. But sorting the bones would be a mammoth enterprise that called for a particular kind of expert—a forensic anthropologist, a scientist who examines bones and other remains to discover information about the life and death of the person to whom they belonged.

Doug Owsley, the division head of physical anthropology at the Smithsonian Institution in Washington, D.C., is one of the world's leading forensic anthropologists. Owsley has examined millions of bones and teeth. He understands how they change with age and use while a person is still alive. Bones become bent, twisted, sometimes broken. Teeth show identifiable patterns of wear and decay from chewing and other tasks. To a trained eye, it becomes easy to separate the bones and teeth of a young person from those of an older person and even to estimate a person's age. The differences among the bones and teeth of the *Hunley's* crew would help Owsley coax each piece into telling its life story.

Several bone experts and medical examiners joined Owsley to sort and reassemble the crew's remains. The scientists examined every feature of the bones and teeth with a microscope or other magnifying device. They matched the bones by size and by how the joints fit together. In about a week, they had separated and laid out eight skeletons.

Although the team felt confident that they had reliably identified Dixon's remains based on their location in the captain's position and the inscribed gold coin found among them, Owsley wanted to investigate further. Rather than assume that any skeleton belonged to any particular crew member, he gave each skeleton a letter name to distinguish it from the others. From bow to stern, the remains were labeled AA through HH, each letter corresponding to an individual skeleton. Thus, the remains found in the captain's position were labeled AA. The man who operated the seventh crank, the closet to the stern of the submarine, was labeled HH.

Owsley's next task was to analyze the remains to learn as much as possible about the crewmen. While examining the left femur of crewman AA—the man presumed to be George Dixon—Owsley found an indentation on the bone's surface and some small particles that tests identified as lead. The gold coin contained similar lead particles. The tests confirmed the story of how a lead bullet had driven the coin into Dixon's thigh, proving that crewman AA was indeed George Dixon.

Owsley discovered that Dixon's crew had been a diverse collection of men. Based on facts known about the *Hunley's* first two crews, archaeologists had expected the final crew to be fairly young. (One of John Payne's crew members had been only twelve or thirteen years old.) Owsley's findings surprised them. Crewman BB was the youngest, between eighteen and twenty-two years old. Crewman FF, the oldest, was in his forties.

Given the *Hunley's* low ceiling, the team also expected that the crewmen would be short. Yet Owsley proved that some of the men were quite tall. Crewman DD was 6 feet 1 inch (1.9 m) tall, while four of the others were 5 feet 10 inches (1.8 m)— all taller than the average height of men serving in the military at that time. Men this size must have found the crew's compartment terribly cramped.

As Owsley assessed the bones' visible features, he saw no evidence of physical trauma that would indicate that the crew had struggled during an attempt to escape from the submarine. As the archaeologists had surmised from the locations and positions of some of the remains, it appeared that the men had died in or near their assigned stations.

Teeth and Bones

After assembling the skeletons and examining them visually, Owsley's team conducted more detailed testing. The team sectioned—cut into thin slices—a portion of one of each man's femurs. To avoid contaminating the sections, the scientists donned surgical gowns, masks, head coverings, and two layers of surgical gloves. The sections would undergo testing to confirm Owsley's age estimates and to provide information about the crewmen's health, diet, and place of origin.

The team also took DNA samples from a femur and a tooth of each crewman with the hope that they might be matched with samples taken from people believed to be relatives of the crew, if such people could be located. DNA—deoxyribonucleic acid—is a basic material found in all living cells. It controls the pattern of inherited characteristics that are passed down from one generation to the next. A specific type of DNA called mitochondrial DNA (mtDNA) is passed from a mother to her children. Only a mother's female children can pass mtDNA on to the following generation. MtDNA can be used to confirm family relationships. A positive mtDNA match between a sample from any crewman's remains and a known relative of that crewman's mother, maternal grandmother, or sister could be used to confirm the crewman's identity.

The mtDNA testing would take months to complete—and first, research had to be done to locate the crewmen's relatives. Meanwhile, Owsley turned his attention to the teeth. "The teeth held some of the most fascinating clues," he recalled. They provided information about the men's habits, diet, and lifestyle. Dark stains on many

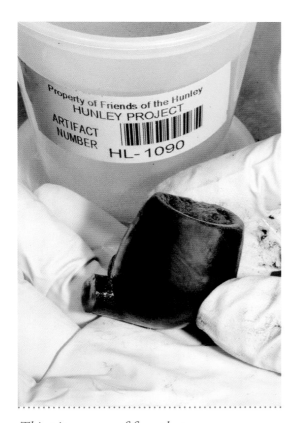

This pipe—one of four that archaeologists found— still contains tobacco.

of the teeth indicated that their owners had chewed tobacco or smoked a pipe. Four men's teeth had curved grooves called facets, which are caused by continuously gripping a pipe stem. This finding matched the archaeologists' discovery of four pipes in the crew's compartment. Crewman CC's teeth had pipe facets so deep that the pulp—the nerve-filled inner section of a tooth—was exposed. He must have almost always had a pipe clamped tightly between his teeth.

A tailor's notch is another type of tooth indentation that Owsley looked for. This notch forms when a needle is regularly gripped between a top and bottom tooth. A tailor's notch is often found on teeth belonging to people who sew frequently, such as tailors (hence the name) and some sailors, who get the notch from holding a needle as they repair a ship's sails.

Owsley found that crewman EE had a tailor's notch. So did crewman DD, but his was oddly placed between two top teeth. Further analysis revealed that he had an overbite; with his mouth closed, his top teeth came down far in front of his bottom teeth. Since he couldn't grip a needle comfortably between a top and bottom tooth, crewman DD had forced his needle between two top teeth. Before these men joined the Hunley's crew, they must have been sailors or had some other occupation in which sewing was a regular part of the job.

Two crewmen—George Dixon and crewman HH—had fillings, some of which were made of gold. During the Civil War era, only fairly wealthy people could afford to pay for gold as filling material. Did these men come from well-to-do families? Owsley noted this possibility for reference later in the investigation.

Tests on the teeth and the thin sections of bone removed from the crewmen's femurs led to the discovery that half of the men were immigrants from Europe. The other crewmen had been born in the United States. How could bones and teeth reveal where a person comes from? A chemical element called carbon is the key. Carbon is absorbed by grains such as corn, wheat, barley, and rye during photosynthesis, the nutrient-making process of green plants. One form of carbon is called carbon 13. Grains that commonly grow in Europe—wheat, barley, and rye—have a smaller amount of carbon 13 than grains that commonly grow in the southern part of North America, such as corn.

When people eat grains, their teeth and bones absorb traces of carbon. Teeth stop absorbing carbon after a person reaches about ten years of age. Bones, in contrast, absorb carbon throughout a person's life. Through scientific testing, Owsley learned that the teeth of four crewmen contained low amounts of carbon 13. This finding indicated that the men had spent at least their first ten years of life in a European country.

The bones of two of the four European crewmen had a slightly larger amount of carbon 13, closer to the amount found in the bones of people who eat North American grains. These men must have lived in North America long enough for their bones to absorb greater amounts of carbon 13. But the bones of the other two European crewmen contained smaller amounts of carbon 13. That indicated that these

Doug Owsley (LEFT) *studies a digital x-ray of a crewman's jawbone.*

men were recent immigrants who hadn't eaten North American grains long enough for their bones to reflect the change in diet.

Owsley's results supplied the team with part of each crewman's story. But the job of identifying the crew members was far from finished. How could the scientists match each skeleton with a name? It was time for Owsley to compare notes with Linda Abrams.

Naming the Crew

As Owsley studied the crew's remains, Linda Abrams had made several promising discoveries, including the identification of direct descendants of James Wicks. However, mtDNA comparisons with Wicks's descendants couldn't be conducted because men don't pass mtDNA to their offspring. Descendants of James Wicks wouldn't have mtDNA that matched his.

But Abrams also located the great-granddaughter of a sister of Joseph Ridgaway. This descendant gave permission for the remains of Joseph's sister to be exhumed, or removed from the ground. This woman's remains would provide a certain mtDNA match with Ridgaway, since both siblings shared their mother's mtDNA.

While this testing took place, Abrams and Owsley reviewed their discoveries. By sharing the information they had gathered, could they successfully pair the crew's remains with specific names? Of the four American crewmen, George Dixon's identity had already been confirmed. Owsley's carbon 13 tests had shown that crewmen DD, GG, and HH had also been born in the United States. Abrams, meanwhile, had discovered that Wicks, Ridgaway, and Collins were Americans as well. These two groups of crewmen must have been one and the same.

Abrams knew that Wicks was an older man who'd had a long career in the navy. Owsley's bone studies showed that crewman GG was about forty-four or forty-five years old. Crewman DD, on the other hand, was only in his twenties—too young to be Wicks. Crewman HH, at age thirty, also seemed too young. It appeared that crewman GG was probably James Wicks.

At this point, the long-awaited mtDNA results proved fruitful. Joseph Ridgaway's identity was confirmed when the mtDNA of crewman HH positively matched the mtDNA results from the exhumed skull of Ridgaway's sister. Thus crewman GG was the only remaining American crewman who was old enough to be James Wicks. By elimination, crewman DD had to be Frank Collins. Using the facts known about the European-born crewmen, Abrams and Owsley followed a similar process to pair each name—Arnold Becker, Corporal J. F. Carlsen, C. Lumpkin, and Miller—with a set of remains.

The matching of Ridgaway's skeleton with his name brought Abrams back to the mystery of Ezra Chamberlin's identification tag, which had been found on Ridgaway's remains. Abrams had already determined that Chamberlin wasn't present on the *Hunley:* He had died in 1863 during a fierce battle on Morris Island, near Charleston. Was it possible that Ridgaway had been on the island and had found the tag, either on the battlefield or on Chamberlin's body? Collecting identification tags as war booty was a common practice among soldiers on both sides of the conflict.

Abrams couldn't determine whether Ridgaway had been on Morris Island. But she did confirm that another *Hunley* crewman, J. F. Carlsen, had been there during the battle. Could Carlsen have acquired Chamberlin's tag and given or sold it to Ridgaway? No one knows. This mystery may never be solved.

COMING TO LIFE

With each crewman identified, matching a face to each of the eight sets of remains would help complete the effort to restore the men's humanity. Then the crew could be laid to rest with their stories told as fully as possible. Unfortunately, no photographs of the crew are known to exist. Since history couldn't supply photographic evidence, the team once again turned to science. Doug Owsley joined with anthropologist Diane France and forensic artist Sharon Long to reconstruct the crewmen's faces.

"The skull provides the outline for us," Doug Owsley explained. By studying human skulls, anthropologists have learned that certain bone features correspond with certain facial features. Closely spaced eye sockets correspond with closely set eyes, for example. A long, humped nasal bridge suggests that its owner had a hooked nose. Broad cheekbones indicate a wide face, while a prominent lower jaw may be a sign of a jutting chin. Anthropologists and forensic artists can use this information to create a lifelike facial reconstruction based on a skull alone.

The first step in this process is to make a rubber form called a mold. Diane France is an expert at making molds of bones. Her job was to make a two-part mold of each crewman's skull by painting layers of a rubbery material called silicone onto one half of a skull. The silicone oozed into openings, tiny cracks, and uneven spaces. After the rubber dried, France peeled it off the bone, then repeated the process with the other half of the skull. To stiffen the slightly floppy mold, she applied putty and plaster to the mold's outer surface. When combined, the two mold halves provide a complete record of the skull's surface details.

Making a replica, also called a cast, of the skull is the next step. France poured a soft plastic mixture into the mold. In about thirty minutes, the plastic hardened and the mold could be removed. The resulting cast was an exact copy of the skull. Even after the planned burial of the crew's remains, anthropologists would be able to rely on the casts for further study.

At this point, artist Sharon Long placed small pegs on the cast to represent the thickness of the tissue and muscles that formerly covered the skull. Long gauged the length and placement of each peg based on both her knowledge of facial anatomy and data supplied by Doug Owsley. Using strips of modeling clay to fill in for tissue and muscles, Long gradually fleshed out the skull.

Some facial features, such as the thickness of lips and the shape of ears, can't be determined by skull features. These details were left to Long to select. Taking each crewman's age into account, she sculpted wrinkles and lines into the clay to

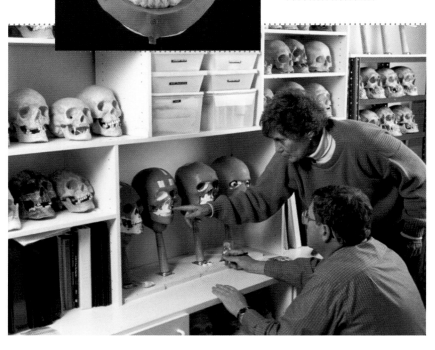

LEFT: *An early stage in the facial reconstruction of crewman BB, Arnold Becker*

BELOW: *Owsley and Long discuss the next steps for four of the crew's facial reconstructions.*

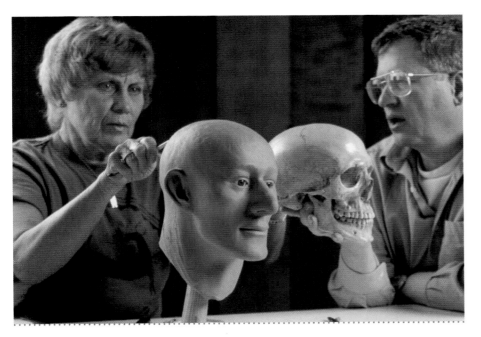

Long carefully shapes clay as Arnold Becker's reconstruction nears completion.

make each face as realistic as possible. She also painted each skull to create the appearance of skin, choosing tones common to white men of American or northern European origin.

Long also chose hair color and eye color for each face except George Dixon's. A person who knew Dixon had described him in a letter as having blond hair and blue eyes. Hair that was found with Dixon's remains was light blond, confirming this aspect of his appearance, so Long completed his facial reconstruction accordingly. To create realistic hairstyles, she chose wigs modeled on styles from the Civil War era. Glass eyeballs, some colored to show blood vessels, were used for the eyes.

Doug Owsley offered details to make the faces more authentic and individual. For example, he suggested placing a pipe in the mouth of C. Lumpkin (crewman CC) and a needle in the tailor's notch of Frank Collins (crewman DD). He also suggested beards and mustaches appropriate for each man's age, based on photographs of Civil War soldiers.

By bringing together their talents, Owsley, Abrams, France, and Long have introduced to the world eight men who courageously volunteered to operate a risky new technology—one that had already killed thirteen men—and ultimately sacrificed their lives in battle.

THE FINAL CREW OF THE *H. L. Hunley*

Lieutenant George E. Dixon
(crewman AA, 24–25 years old)

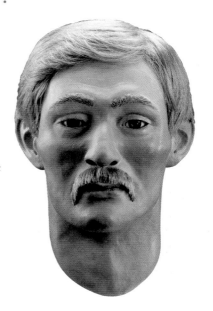

The men of the Twenty-First Alabama Infantry Regiment regarded Dixon as "the best kind of fellow." His bravery in battle led to his rapid promotion to lieutenant. Dixon shared boxes of treats with his fellow soldiers and gladly joined fishing trips to catch a meal tastier than army rations. His letters show that he was an educated man. He wore expensive jewelry and clothes—fiber analysis showed that one of his garments was made of cashmere. Carbon testing proved that Dixon was born in the United States but wasn't originally from the South. His birthplace and family are unknown.

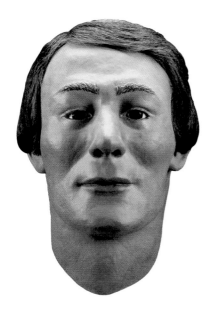

Arnold Becker
(crewman BB, 19–22 years old)

Becker was the youngest and, at 5 feet 6 inches (1.7 m), the shortest crewman. But he had huge responsibilities. Dixon trusted him enough to place him at the first crank handle, where he functioned as Dixon's assistant. Becker operated the forward pump, the snorkel tubes, and the bellows. Carbon tests revealed he was born in Europe and had recently immigrated to the United States. He worked on a riverboat out of New Orleans, where he signed on to the Confederate navy after the war began. Becker's birthplace and family remain unknown.

C. Lumpkin
(crewman CC, 37–45 years old)

Lumpkin operated the second crank handle. Carbon tests indicated that he was born in Europe but had lived in the United States for a long time before he died. Before joining the crew of the *Hunley,* he served on the CSS *Indian Chief,* the ship stationed in Charleston Harbor from which George Dixon sought volunteers. He may have had a reputation as a tough fighter. Owsley theorizes that healed fractures in Lumpkin's nasal bone and upper jaw could have been the result of a fistfight. Lumpkin's first name, birthplace, and family remain unknown.

Frank Collins
(crewman DD, 23–26 years old)

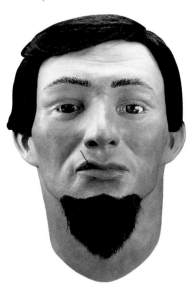

Collins was the tallest man on the crew. Sitting at the *Hunley's* third crank handle must have been a tight squeeze for him. His job was simply to crank as hard as possible toward the submarine's target. Collins was born in Fredericksburg, Virginia. After his mother died when he was a boy, he and his brother, John, were raised in their grandparents' home. Collins may have developed his tailor's notch from working with his grandfather, a shoemaker. In the Confederate navy records, he is listed as a "seaman." This meant he had experience sailing on ocean water. Collins has no known descendants.

Corporal J. F. Carlsen
(crewman EE, 20–23 years old)

Carlsen operated the fourth crank handle in the seat from which escape was least likely. This young man had a sense of adventure. He served as a helmsman on the *Jeff Davis,* an infamous privateer. (Privateers were privately owned ships that captured Union vessels for their cargo. The sailors received a share of the profits.) Later, as a Confederate soldier, he received a special commendation for courage under fire. He joined the *Hunley's* crew after William Alexander was reassigned to Mobile. Carlsen was born in Europe and, like Collins, had a tailor's notch. His first name, birthplace, and family remain unknown.

Miller
(crewman FF, 40–47 years old)

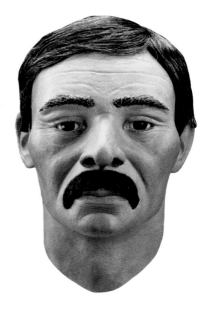

Miller, who worked the fifth crank handle, is mentioned only by last name in the historical record. Carbon testing showed that he was born in Europe, then moved to the United States. He may have had a difficult life: His leg bones showed traces of disease, and at some point before joining the *Hunley* crew, he'd broken a leg and a rib and had fractured his skull. He was missing molars and had deep pipe facets in his teeth as well. Other than these few bits of information, nothing is known about this crewman.

James A. Wicks
(crewman GG, 44–45 years old)

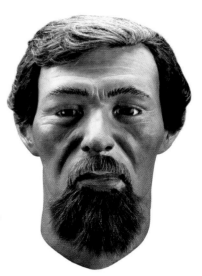

Wicks is the only crewman known to have living direct descendants. Born in North Carolina, he was a U.S. Navy sailor who enlisted in the Confederate navy after the Civil War began. He served as a commando on a secret raid to free a ship and a North Carolina port from Union control. The ship was captured by the commando group, but under fierce fire from Union troops, the raid ultimately failed. By mid-February, Wicks had returned to Charleston and resumed his battle station behind the sixth crank handle.

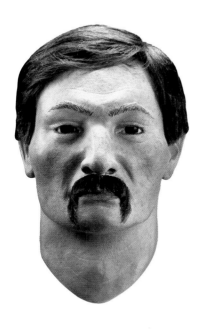

Joseph Ridgaway
(crewman HH, 30 years old)

Ridgaway was raised in Talbot County, Maryland. His father owned several ships as well as a small plantation. The family's wealth explains the presence of the gold filling that Owsley found in one of Ridgaway's teeth. By the time Ridgaway was sixteen, he had earned his Seaman's Protection Certificate, which established his qualifications as a sailor with experience on the open ocean. In addition to working the seventh crank handle on the *Hunley*, he was responsible for the aft seacock and ballast tank pump. Ridgaway was wearing Ezra Chamberlin's identification tag around his neck when the *Hunley* sank.

Unsolved Mysteries

By the end of 2003, the excavation of the *Hunley* was complete. Hundreds of bones, more than three thousand artifacts, and 20,000 pounds (9,000 kg) of sediment had been removed from the submarine.

The *Hunley* team has solved some mysteries, but others remain. Did the submarine sink? If so, why? Or was it piloted intentionally to the seafloor? How did the crew perish?

The team is considering several possible ways the *Hunley* might have sunk. Stratigraphic evidence has ruled out the two large breaches in the hull as the cause of such an event. But what about the grapefruit-sized hole in the forward conning tower? Could a gunshot from the *Housatonic* have made this hole? Or was it created after the submarine sank, perhaps in a manner similar to the two larger holes? For now, scientists believe that the hole was made after the submarine sank and the crewmen's

A view of the submarine's interior after the excavation

bodies had decomposed. If the hole had been present while the bodies were decomposing, crabs would have scuttled inside, searching for food. No crab shells were found inside the submarine.

The conning tower hatches have provided additional clues. The aft hatch was closed and locked down into position. The forward hatch, where Dixon stood, was closed, but not locked down. After the *Hunley* backed away from the *Housatonic,* did Dixon open the hatch to watch the Union ship sink, to let in fresh air, or to use the signal lantern? If so, could a wave have swamped the submarine?

Among the team's remaining tasks is the x-raying of the hull and all of the machinery. With the sediment removed, x-rays should show exactly what lies beneath the layers of concretion on the hull and the machinery. It's possible that the concretion may be hiding a crack or other defect that caused the submarine to sink.

After thorough study, the concretion still in place over much of the submarine's machinery will be removed, allowing close examination of the seacocks. Is either one open? An open seacock would have allowed water to flood the crew's compartment— the same fate suffered by Horace Hunley's crew.

While it seems unlikely that Dixon's crew would repeat such a grave mistake, another possibility exists. During a speech in 1902, William Alexander recalled the frightening test dive in which seaweed had clogged his ballast pump. After that scare, he said, he and Dixon discussed what they would do if they ever again found themselves unable to surface. Knowing that they would rather drown than await death by suffocation in the dark submarine, they agreed to deliberately open the seacocks. Might this have occurred?

Some of the submarine's internal concretion has been removed already, revealing unexpected clues. In July 2004, archaeologists uncovered a series of previously unknown valves and pumps in the forward and aft sections of the crew compartment. A pipe that runs between the two ballast tanks is connected to the valves and pumps. Could this system have enabled the crew to remove water from their compartment in the event of an unexpected flood? If so, the position of the valves could reveal whether the crew faced such a situation during their final moments. The team will learn more after conservators remove the concretion from the valves.

Scientists will also continue to analyze the positions of the pieces found outside the *Hunley* before she was raised. Determining when the cutwater, the snorkel tubes, and the rudder broke off could help reveal the sequence of events that occurred as the *Hunley* sank. For example, it's possible that the rudder broke off when the submarine shoved against the bottom during an intentional descent. If so, the damage may have affected Dixon's ability to ascend. It's also possible that the rudder broke long after the *Hunley* sank; water currents may have shifted and wedged it under the submarine.

Along with these investigations and the study of Dixon's pocket watch, Scott Harris's ongoing stratigraphic analysis may help answer the team's questions. Minute particles such as grains of plant pollen may reveal the seasons when the various sediment layers were deposited. This information could be linked to the timing of the sinking and its possible causes.

Some evidence already gathered, while intriguing, remains inconclusive. Arnold Becker, whose body Maria Jacobsen found concreted to the bellows, was the only one not at his crank handle, which would have been the first crank. Had he left the handle to operate the forward ballast pump, perhaps in an attempt to stop flooding?

On the other hand, the positions of the other crewmen don't indicate a mad scramble to escape a flooding submarine. Six men appear to have died in battle positions, each near his own crank handle. Had these men sat peacefully as the submarine descended, only losing consciousness and suffocating after she reached the seafloor? Or had water rapidly filled the submarine and drowned the men before they could move—maybe before the submarine even hit the bottom?

Another clue reinforces the theory that the crew lacked the time or the capacity to react to whatever disaster struck the *Hunley*. The detachable iron ballast weights remained bolted to the keel. Had the men had the desire and opportunity to ascend quickly, they would have very likely loosened these bars.

After the team's years of meticulous work, is it frustrating to face so many unanswered questions? On the contrary, the scientists remain determined. As Harry Pecorelli observes, "Different disciplines have come together to tell the whole story. I think we stand a better chance today of telling what happened to the crew and the submarine than if the submarine had been brought up [in 1864]."

Maria Jacobsen echoes his confidence. "When all is said and done," she predicts, "I'm fairly comfortable that we will be able to tell exactly what happened to the submarine and crew. It just takes time."

REST IN PEACE

George Dixon's crew had begun their courageous mission on a cold, wintry night in 1864. They completed their final voyage on the warm, sunny afternoon of April 17,

2004. During a solemn ceremony at the Battery, a Charleston park, World War II submarine veterans carried the crew's caskets as a show of respect for the men who had paved the way for future submariners. Afterward, thousands of onlookers watched respectfully as eight horse-drawn caissons carried the men's remains to Charleston's Magnolia Cemetery. The members of the *Hunley's* final crew were buried with full military honors alongside the graves of those who had served on the submarine before them.

A proper military funeral marked the passing of the Hunley *crewmen, 140 years after their deaths.*

While her crew rests in Magnolia Cemetery, the *Hunley's* voyage continues. Archaeologists and conservators will not cease their work until she and every artifact found inside her have been thoroughly studied and safely preserved. Plans are under way for the construction of a museum in North Charleston where the submarine and her artifacts will be permanently displayed.

As the first submarine to sink an enemy ship, the *Hunley* holds a unique place in history. She and her crew changed the course of naval combat in much the same way that the Wright Brothers changed the course of aviation. The *Hunley's* achievement inspired engineers to pursue further innovations in undersea warfare. Even so, it

A horse-drawn caisson transports George Dixon's remains to their final resting place.

wasn't until more than fifty years later, during World War I, that her successful underwater attack was repeated by another submarine.

James McClintock and the other men who built the *Hunley* created a technological marvel the likes of which the world had never seen. George Dixon and his crew staked her claim as a weapon of destruction. The members of the *Hunley* team are securing her yet another place in history. Since Harry Pecorelli first touched her in 1995, the *Hunley* has become an instrument of instruction. She provokes scientists to develop new investigative techniques. She challenges historians to delve deeper into our record of the past. The *Hunley* dares people of all ages to savor history and delight in science. She teaches everyone the value of a good story. And like the very best of storytellers, she spins her tale slowly, one chapter at a time. We're still waiting for her conclusion.

A Note from the Author

For me, doing research is like opening a door into a fascinating new world. Often it's a world of libraries and letters, photographs and diaries. At the National Archives in Washington, D.C.—a treasure chest of untold stories about the United States and its people—I held and read original documents, handwritten by people who had seen the *Hunley* and her crew in action. Each note connected me, in a personal way, to its author. As I read the words of George Dixon and the testimonies of the *Housatonic* survivors, I felt like another witness to that history-making month of February 1864.

In South Carolina, too, I found many traces of the past. At the South Carolina Historical Society in Charleston, Nic Butler and Pat Kruger helped me examine letters and other period documents that related to the *Hunley*. Brian Hicks, author of *Raising the Hunley*, suggested that I visit Adger's Wharf, where Horace Hunley and his crew had docked on the morning of their deaths. As I sat on the wharf, watching the black porpoises in the harbor, I understood exactly why Emma Holmes had called the *Hunley* an "iron porpoise."

I experienced the same sense of connection in the other world of the *Hunley*, that of the modern scientists and historians whose aims are to preserve and protect the submarine and to honor her history. Glenn McConnell, chairman of the *Hunley* Commission, graciously explained the intricacies of her ownership and the unique challenges her recovery presented. Through many telephone interviews and e-mails, Linda Abrams and Scott Harris introduced me to George Dixon's crew and helped me interpret the submarine's stratigraphy. Harry Pecorelli answered questions, vetted the text, and offered feedback to scientific illustrator Laura Westlund, who created the diagrams and maps in this book.

During my time in North Charleston, Maria Jacobsen gave me a personal tour of the *Hunley* and her environs at the Warren Lasch Conservation Center. From the research I'd already done, I knew the submarine was just under 40 feet long and a few feet tall. Even so, I was startled by how small she is. I couldn't help wondering: Had I lived in 1864, would I have had the nerve to climb aboard?

Being a writer, I loved watching one of the *Hunley* conservators clean a pencil. Claire Peachey also showed me shoes, pencils, and other artifacts excavated from the wreck of the *Housatonic*. (And yes, I had to wear surgical gloves while examining them!) Doug Owsley welcomed me to the Smithsonian Institution, where I spent a day looking at forensic slides and reading his field notes describing the crew's remains.

I also heard many personal stories from people whose lives have been touched by the *Hunley*. In Virginia, Sally Necessary, Queen Bennett's great-granddaughter, shared family history and pictures of her ancestor. I enjoyed learning about crewman James Wicks from his great-great-granddaughter, Mary Elizabeth McMahon. Edgar "Mac" McCollum, volunteer extraordinaire at the Lasch Center, enthralled me with his tales of life in a World War II submarine and answered many questions about submarines and buoyancy. I was proud to stand near him on April 17, 2004, as he served as a pallbearer for *Hunley* crewman Frank Collins.

I always feel slightly sad when a good story ends—like I'm saying good-bye to a friend I may not see again for a long time. Fortunately, this story isn't over yet. I'll be watching with the *Hunley's* many other fans to see what secrets she reveals next.

Source Notes

Page 11 Dabney H. Maury, "How the Confederacy Changed Naval Warfare," *Southern Historical Society Papers* 22 (1894): 79.

14 William A. Alexander, "The True Stories of the Confederate Submarine Boats," *New Orleans Picayune,* 29 June 1902.

23 Emma Holmes, *The Diary of Miss Emma Holmes 1861-1866,* ed. John F. Marszalek (Baton Rouge, LA: Louisiana State University Press, 1979), 302.

23–24 *The War of the Rebellion: A Compilation of the Official Records of the Union and Confederate Armies* (1880; reprint, Gettysburg, PA: National Historical Society, 1972), 28: 670.

24 "A Miraculous Escape," newspaper clipping (n.p., n.d., 1898 or earlier by context), Augustine Thomas Smythe Papers, South Carolina Historical Society, Charleston, SC.

25 Ibid.

25 Ibid.

25 C. L. Stanton, "Submarines and Torpedo Boats," *Confederate Veteran* 22 (13 Sept. 1914): 398.

25 *War of the Rebellion,* 551.

28 Ibid., 145.

28 Stanton, 398.

30 Pierre G. T. Beauregard, "Torpedo Service in the Harbor and Water Defences [sic] of Charleston," *Southern Historical Society Papers* 5 (1878): 153.

30 Pierre G. T. Beauregard to George E. Dixon, 5 November 1863, Letters and Telegrams Sent, First Military District, Department of South Carolina, Georgia, and Florida, 1863-1864, Record Group 109, National Archives, Washington, D.C.

31–32 William Alexander, "Thrilling Chapter in the History of the Confederate States Navy," *Southern Historical Society Papers* 30 (1902): 169.

33 George E. Dixon to Henry Willey, 31 January, 1864, *Charleston Post and Courier,* 11 April 2004, 6A.

33 William Alexander, "Thrilling Chapter," 170.

33 Dixon to Willey, 6A.

33 William Alexander, "Thrilling Chapter," 171.

33–34 Ibid.

36 "Proceedings of the Naval Court of Inquiry," 26 February, 1864, Case #4345, Record Group 45, National Archives, Washington D.C.

36 Ibid.

37 Ibid.

37–38 *War of the Rebellion* 35: 262

42 Harry Pecorelli III, interview by author, North Charleston, SC, 24 July 2003.

42 Ibid.

42 Ibid.

43 Ibid.

45 Claire Peachy, interview by author, Washington, D.C., 7 August 2003.

50 Maria Jacobsen, interview by author, North Charleston, SC, 24 July 2003.

53 Pecorelli, interview.

55 Jacobsen, interview.

58 Ibid.

62 Ibid.

69 Maria Jacobsen, e-mail to author, 24 May 2004.

78 Pecorelli, interview.

81 Jacobsen, interview.

83 Ibid.

84 Ibid.

86 Pecorelli, interview.

86 Linda Abrams, telephone conversation with author, 19 December 2003.

90 Doug Owsley, public lecture, Charleston, SC, 13 April 2004.

95 Ibid.

98 James M. Williams, *From That Terrible Field: Civil War Letters of James M. Williams, Twenty-First Alabama Infantry Volunteers,* ed. John Kent Folmar (Tuscaloosa, AL: University of Alabama Press, 1981), 47.

105 Pecorelli, interview.

106 Jacobsen, interview.

Selected Bibliography

Bak, Richard. *The CSS Hunley.* Dallas, TX: Taylor Publishing Co., 1999.

Campbell, R. Thomas. *The CSS H. L. Hunley.* Shippensburg, PA: Burd Street Press, 2000.

Geier, Clarence R., and Stephen R. Potter, editors. *Archaeological Perspectives on the American Civil War.* Gainesville, FL: University Press of Florida, 2000.

Hicks, Brian, and Schuyler Kropf. *Raising the Hunley.* New York: Ballantine Books, 2002.

Oeland, Glen. *"Secret Weapon of the Confederacy."* National Geographic (July 2002): 82-101.

Porter, David D. *The Naval History of the Civil War.* New York: Sherman Publishing Company, 1886.

Ragan, Mark K. *The Hunley: Submarines, Sacrifice, & Success in the Civil War.* Charleston, SC: Narwhal Press, 1999.

Ragan, Mark K. *Submarine Warfare in the Civil War.* Cambridge, MA: Da Capo Press, 2002.

Schafer, Louis S. *Confederate Underwater Warfare: An Illustrated History.* Jefferson, NC: McFarland & Co., 1996.

Websites

CSS Hunley, *National Underwater and Marine Agency* <http://www.numa.net/expeditions/hunley.html>

Friends of the Hunley <http://www.hunley.org>

Photo Acknowledgments

All photographs © 2005 Friends of the *Hunley*® except: PhotoDisc Royalty Free by Getty Images, water images on endsheets and p. 1; National Archives, pp. 6 (NWDNS-111-B-744), 8 (NWDNS-165-C-751), 23 (Old Military Records, Hunley, Unfiled papers RG109, Entry M-347), 27 (Old Military Records, Horace L. Hunley, Confederate Papers relating to Citizens or Business Firms, RG 109 Entry M-346), 31 (Old Military Records, Dixon to General Jordan Letters Received, Depart. of SC, GA & FL, 1862-1864, RG 109); United States Navy Submarine Warfare Division, p. 9; Naval Historical Center, pp. 10 (left) (NH95279), 37 (NH53573), 40 (NH53544); Library of Congress (LC-USZC2-2520), p. 22 ; Courtesy of George Bennett Walker, Jr. and Sally Walker Necessary, Great-Grandchildren of Queen Bennett Walker, p. 29; © courtesy of The Museum of Mobile, p. 32; from the original painting by Mort Künstler, *The Final Mission*, © 2003 Mort Künstler, Inc., www.mkunstler.com, p. 35; © 2005 Friends of the *Hunley*®, courtesy of Doug Owsley, photos by Chip Clark, pp. 92, 96 (both), 97; © Sally M. Walker, p. 107.

Glossary

AFT: toward the back end of a water-going vessel

ANTHROPOLOGY: the scientific study of human beings and their cultures

ARCHAEOLOGY: the scientific study of the material remains of past human beings and their cultures

ARTIFACT: an object made by people

BALLAST: material used to improve the stability and affect the ascent and descent of a water-going vessel

BOW: the front end of a water-going vessel

CONCRETION: particles of matter, previously separate, that have solidified into a single mass

CONSERVATION: preserving an object from deterioration

FORWARD: toward the front end of a water-going vessel

GENEALOGY: the study of family origins, history, and ancestry

HULL: the main body of a water-going vessel

IN SITU: in the exact location in which an object was found

MATERIALS SCIENCE: the study of the properties of materials

MITOCHONDRIAL DNA: genetic material passed on from a mother to her children. Also known as mtDNA.

PORT: when facing the front of a water-going vessel, the left side

SEDIMENT: particles such as clay, sand, silt, and animal and plant remains that settle out of moving water

STARBOARD: when facing the front of a water-going vessel, the right side

STERN: the back end of a water-going vessel

STRATIGRAPHY: the study of sediment layers. This term is also used to describe such layers themselves.

Index